A SPIRITUAL
AWAKENING

A SPIRITUAL
AWAKENING

How to Respond to the Emerging
HUNGER FOR GOD

TOMMIE ZITO

Destiny Image® Publishers, Inc.
P.O. Box 310
Shippensburg, PA 17257-0310

*"Speaking to the Purposes of God for This Generation
and for the Generations to Come"*

ISBN 0-7684-2250-7

For Worldwide Distribution
Printed in the U.S.A.

This book and all other Destiny Image, Revival Press, MercyPlace,
Fresh Bread, Destiny Image Fiction, and Treasure House books are available
at Christian bookstores and distributors worldwide.

1 2 3 4 5 6 7 8 9 10 / 09 08 07 06 05 04

For a U.S. bookstore nearest you, call
1-800-722-6774.

For more information on foreign distributors, call
717-532-3040.

Or reach us on the Internet:
www.destinyimage.com

DEDICATION

This book is dedicated to my father, Thomas Zito (1927-1996) who laid the foundation for a true follower of Jesus Christ. He walked in the spirit of David and I will forever be grateful for his legacy. Thousands of lives were changed from the faithfulness of this simple man sent from heaven. He showed the power that one vessel could have for the Kingdom if truly yielded to the Spirit. Only heaven will know the true impact of his life here on the earth. He was an ordinary man with an extraordinary God.

ACKNOWLEDGMENTS

First I want to thank my amazing wife, Kimberly, who has walked right with me in this cry for the harvest daily. Your faithfulness for this revival and this team has set an incredible example for many. Remember, the rewards are greater than the sacrifices, and all your rewards are on their way. Thanks for being a great woman of faith, partner, mother, and friend.

I also want to thank my staff editor Holly Gray. I always thought acknowledgments were sappy especially when they read, "I could not have done it without them." Yet here I am writing the same things. You have been an incredible writing partner and I believe your books on this move of Heaven will be read by millions, and if the Lord tarries generations to come. Thanks for devoting countless late-night hours, and even some nights with no sleep, to do what you do for this team. Eternal destinies will be changed forever.

Finaly I want to thank the entire staff of Tommie Zito Ministries. You are the best group of followers of Christ to work with. Thanks for crying out with me day and night. Together we will see another American awakening.

TABLE OF CONTENTS

FOREWORD

This book on a spiritual awakening comes right from the heart of Evangelist Tommie Zito. Tommie has a passion for the lost, an extreme hunger for God, and a deep love for America. I pray that as you read this book it will stir you, awaken you, and put a fire and a hunger in you for revival and for the next great Spiritual Awakening.

This book is a call for the American church to wake up and come out of religion and tradition and realize the urgency of the hour. This is the time to give ALL for the CALL. The harvest is ripe, but it's going to take those who are full of the fire of God, in this hour, to see America shaken. This is a call to war; a time for the army of God in America to rise up and see America shaken.

It has been my privilege to be able to speak into Tommie's life for the last eight years and there is no doubt in my mind that God will use Tommie in the future to shake whole regions of the world. Get ready—because we stand on the brink of the next great Spiritual Awakening!

Dr. Rodney M. Howard-Browne
Tampa, Florida October 2004

INTRODUCTION

WHAT DOES IT MEAN TO HAVE AN AWAKENING?

Parents are entrusted by the Lord to raise children and discipline them according to His Word. Raising children is hardly an easy undertaking, and the everyday responsibility of bringing up kids can be overwhelming.

I can remember my father waking me up as a young boy for school each day. The routine was the same every morning, and I remember it as if it were yesterday. My father would approach my bedroom door and gently knock, calling in a moderate tone of voice, "Tommie, it's time to get up." I recall hearing him speak those words but I was in no way motivated to act on them. They were dreaded words that brought a feeling of discomfort. My bed, on the other hand, was comfortable. It seemed to embrace me, and I was in no hurry to remove myself from its warmth. My family found it efficient not to use heat in the mornings, so leaving those blankets to get up to take a shower was not something that excited me.

Often, my normal response was, "Dad, please give me a few more minutes." I said those words in the softest and kindest voice I could muster, begging for more time. I did anything to put off the agony. My dad was gracious, knowing my routine all too well, and he always called me early enough so I would have sufficient time to prepare for the day. He was my snooze alarm.

Once again, I would let the comfort of my bed take hold. Sleep would overcome me, and I considered myself in the clear.

But what seemed like seconds later, a giant tempest blast hit my bedroom as loud as you could ever imagine with a deafening shout, "GET UP NOW! IT'S TIME!" My father meant business. There was no more playing around. Friends who often stayed over at my house said that they never heard anything like it before. In an instant, I was suddenly wide-awake and ready for the day. The comfort of my bed became quickly uncomfortable. The warmth of the covers no longer enticed me. I was awake—wide-awake. In a similar way, I believe that this book contains the elements of what it takes to have an awakening, a wide-awakening. I pray that as you read, your heart and mind will be open to all God desires to do in you and through you.

THE MANDATE OF THIS MINISTRY

Nobody looks forward to hearing the sound of an alarm clock. It is probably one of the worst sounds we hear all day. Although not one of the most popular of home appliances, it is, however, the most necessary. It signals the time to prepare for what lies ahead. Whether it is to go to work or school, the purpose remains the same—it serves to get us up on time! The words in this book have the ability to become just that for you, but you must allow them to penetrate.

In the history of the church and various spiritual movements, God has used a variety of ways or methods to wakeup people. You can learn about them by taking some time to study spontaneous revivals that have sprung up all over the world. Unfortunately, I believe the church as a whole has brought itself to the place where it is constantly hitting a spiritual snooze button and asking for a few more minutes to sleep. While it may be continuing to slumber comfortably, I believe the Lord will soon be setting off an earsplitting detonation.

This book is written from my perspective as a young evangelist who cannot fathom how the church system has been debased. I will pull no punches. I will express my heart and expose many things I have seen in the American church today that must be disposed of quickly. I believe in what I am saying.

My prayer is that this book will take the scales off your eyes so that you may behold the truths and embrace them. I also pray that it will inflame your heart so that you will become passionate for the lost souls in our nation and turn from any state of mediocrity that exists within you. May you approach this book with an openness to receive correction, or conviction, if it may be, and humbly bow on your knees with a heart of repentance. Unless we repent as a people, many will miss the awakening that is essential to our lives. What I write about is not just theories or ideas that I have stumbled upon. No. These are things that have been proven and that I have personally witnessed for the past several years.

We are beginning to see the birth of a spiritual awakening. Although currently in its infancy stage, it is progressing rapidly. Christians who have been dormant for years are waking up to the power of God and proclaiming their faith every day in public venues. God will not fully bless this land until things change. He hates hypocrisy and the American church is full of it, beginning with its leaders. The lack of hunger and passion that I have witnessed in leaders is resounding. I am surprised that many pastors and other church leaders have the audacity to stand in the pulpit as shepherds who are supposed to care for their sheep.

After reading this book, you may come to the conclusion that I just want to bash the church. Please guard your heart and realize that our ministry loves the church. We are in churches every day of the week, most times twice a day. We conduct over 500 revival meetings a year. We love the church, and true love does what is best for someone. A true friend will tell you the truth even when he knows that what he says might hurt you. The good news is that thousands have already received this message from Heaven and have been hit by the blast and awakened into a glorious conversion to Christ and His fullness. When the world sees true Christianity, they will fall in love with Jesus.

The question that constantly comes to mind is this: Where are the passionate followers of Christ, similar to those who are mentioned throughout the Bible, who ran wholeheartedly after

God and walked with the confidence and authority given them? Where are those individuals who grab hold of God's promises and base their lives on what He says? Gandhi himself was quoted as saying, "I would have been a Christian had I ever seen one." There are people in counseling sessions after counseling sessions, depending on words they hear from individuals before they seek counseling from the true Counselor Himself. There are people who come into church meeting after church meeting seeking prayer. Their motives may be pure, but unless they grasp the truths found in God's Word and believe—just believe what He says—the capacity for change becomes minute.

It is easy to complain and share our hurts and disappointments with one another. We find it comforting to bring our broken hearts and wounds to individuals who we feel have experienced the same things. But why is it that we run to others to fix us? Why is it that the first person we often go to is not God? Where does our confidence lie? Our focus should not be on the circumstances and situations we are faced with, but in the God who is in control of the circumstances—the God who gave His all for *you*! As Christians, when faced with troublesome situations, nothing should move us. Where the flesh may become weak, we can turn to Someone inside who is greater.

Why is it that people fail to see their full potential in God? We need to be reminded of who we are to Him. Many of us are not scratching even the surface of what God wants to do in and through us. When faced with unexpected events in life, we need to understand that we have been crucified with Christ. Regardless of what may come against you, nothing should move you...be it anything from criticism to persecution...there is nothing that takes place in your life that has the ability to separate you from the love of Jesus...no height, no depth...nothing!

As a Christian, I challenge you to be the unshakeable, unmovable child God desires you to be. Establish yourself on the Rock of Jesus Christ. Allow your mind to be fixed on the eternal so that you walk in the supernatural and in the glory. Decide that no matter what, God will get the glory. When the storms of life come, make sure that your house is built on the Rock and not the sand. Resolve that you will make it through the storm, tried and true and in complete victory!

As this mighty revival sweeps across America, many will embrace a new perspective of their role as a believer. Many will come to realize the position given to them as a child of God and walk in it. Millions will be touched and awakened, and we will see the great end-time harvest of souls that has been promised.

Chapter One

THE OBEDIENCE
OF ONE VESSEL

He spent hours upon hours reading the Word. Day after day, night after night, He talked with the One whom he loved the most. His time was consumed with sharing the gospel, and he literally took every opportunity he could to tell others the Good News. He was desperate for God. He was a real Christian.

Traveling with our ministry, I've met few Christians who truly care about souls and the harvest. People would rather talk about who won last night's football game, religion, or politics than things of eternal value—not so for Dad.

My dad lived life as a real Christian. He made the most of every day, living for the purpose of his call, and living that way always presented opportunities to share the gospel. I remember heading down to breakfast one morning, passing Dad on my way to the kitchen. Suddenly, I recalled a question I needed to ask him, but as soon as I turned to find him, he was gone.

Where was Dad? He was standing on our street corner sharing the gospel with a Jehovah Witness before the Jehovah Witness had a chance to knock on our door. Dad never waited for an opportunity; he found it before it came to him. There was a time Dad was admitted to a heart institute in New Jersey for one week. There were 10 individuals admitted to each floor. All nine other patients on his floor accepted Jesus, three of whom died the following week. Even in the hospital with tubes going through his nose, he walked the hallways and shared his faith. He seized every opportunity to share the gospel, no matter where he was or what he was doing.

HUNGER IN YOUTH

As I grew up in an Assemblies of God church, the things of the Holy Spirit were alive and fresh in me, and I had such a hunger for Him. Regrettably, however, I found the youth group I attended somewhat discouraging. Because the group was full of teenage boys and girls, the youth group leaders were always scrambling to find things that would fill our minds with fun and keep us out of trouble. We always ended up playing Chutes and Ladders, or maybe some darts, or even ventured out to the bowling lanes. It was really quite distasteful to me. What amazes me now is that years later, our youth groups still embrace these concepts. The only difference is that Chutes and Ladders and the bowling dates have been replaced with pizza parties, sega games, and x-box. At least half of youth group time is spent socializing, while there are teenage hearts searching for more.

We need a move of God in our youth groups. I am not talking about a little Bible study and some Scripture being quoted every once in a while. I am talking about a revival among our young people. They are so very desperate and hungry. The holes in their hearts are longing to be filled, and it is up to the church to fill them with the things of God so that the world looses its grip on their lives. Youth groups should not be one big social club. It is a shame, and it grieves me every time I talk about it. Bowling is fine, but it doesn't solve any problems or pressures that teenagers face. They need something genuine and tangible to lean on. Youth groups need revival.

MY NATURAL *AND* MY SPIRITUAL FATHER

So, for the most part, I would stay away from the youth group and spend time with my father. My natural father became my youth pastor and spiritual father, and he taught me the very things of God. He was the one who encouraged me to begin praying and reading the Bible. I was very close to my father and had a great relationship with him. He was an unbelievable man of God; and he, who had been a full-time minister who won thousands and thousands of people to the Lord, taught me what just one vessel could accomplish.

I can remember waking up at two or three o'clock in the morning, walking downstairs, and seeing my dad travailing in prayer. He wasn't the normal type of father. He enjoyed sports and things, but he enjoyed prayer so much more. Every evening he would retire at about eight o'clock...early, I know; but I never really questioned him about it. He would go upstairs and get on his knees in the presence of God and would pray for hours. It must have been three, four, five, or even six hours every night. No wonder people would be convicted when they came into His presence. Their knees would start to buckle and have fellowship together!

A SELFISH CHRISTIANITY

There were times growing up that I would actually become irritated with my dad. One time when I was in Bible school in Tulsa, Oklahoma, my parents came for a visit. I was very excited about seeing them and spending time together. As we headed downtown for a Chili Fest, it wasn't long before I realized Dad was not walking with us. To be perfectly honest, I was annoyed. I had been looking forward to seeing my dad and spending time with him, but he couldn't be found. I turned around and there a distance back was Dad...and he was doing what he always did—sharing his faith. He was praying for a man who was crying; then he hugged him and put some money in his hand. As I walked to where they were standing, I sensed a glow emanating from them. My attitude and heart instantly changed as I heard Dad's words, "Tommie, those are the ones we have to reach. If we don't reach them, who will?" I could no longer enjoy the Chili Fest. It was not important and neither were my selfish thoughts.

Christianity is selfish; it has become a "me" game. Me, me, me. What about me? What can I get out of it? But we are missing it by a long run. We need to be engulfed in the very essence of His presence and His love for the lost people around us. We need to be intoxicated with the very things that drove Him as He walked on this earth, and we are here to tell them! Recently, on a golf course in Austin, Texas, our pastor met a young man who had never even heard the name of Jesus Christ. He had never heard! How is that possible? What are our churches doing? Are we too concerned with the next coffee hour and our pat-me-on-the-back clubs? Have we over-complicated Christianity with our many denominations and legalistic requirements?

What about the lost and dying world that is waiting for an answer? An answer that we have, and are required to go and tell. When life is over, there is only one thing that matters. It is very simple. Heaven or hell.

ONE YIELDED VESSEL

Romans 5:19 says, "For as by one man's disobedience many were made sinners, so by the obedience of one shall many be made righteous" (KJV). The New Living Translation says it this way, "Because one person disobeyed God, many people became sinners. But because one other person obeyed many people will be made right in God's sight." In essence, because of Adam's disobedience, we were all made sinners, but because of the sacrificial love of Jesus, we are being made righteous. Through one vessel, sin was brought into the world, and through another, a way out was made. A price was paid.

I sometimes think that we forget the potential that one person has. Do you realize what lies on the inside of you? Do you realize that you have the ability to make a difference and change the world? The ones who think they can change the world are often the very ones who do. The ones who believe in themselves and who they are in Christ are the ones willing to step out entrusting their vision to God. After all, it is Christ who places those dreams inside of us to begin with. The key is being one yielded vessel.

To yield is to bear or bring forward or to give up the possession of something, basically giving something away.[1] When is the last time you surrendered and completely yielded yourself to God, allowing Him to use you, your gifting, your abilities, and your dreams? When was the last time you let go and said, "God, here I am; use me"? Once you realize your significance and your value to God, you leave room for the extraordinary. Once you yield yourself to God, you will see His own dreams unfold in your life.

Joseph was a dreamer and he entrusted his life in the Dream-Fulfiller. When all looked seemingly bleak in his own life, his God came through. Even when it looked like God had failed him as he sat in prison, God was working on His behalf using his very dreams to bring him to a place of favor.

YOU WERE BORN FOR SUCH A TIME

Speaking of favor, look at Esther. A Jewish orphan girl under the care of Mordecai, her cousin, she was brought to the citadel of Susa to be prepared as a possible queen for the king. Upon entering the palace she was graced with favor. "Now the king was attracted to Esther more than to any of the other women, and she won his favor and approval more than any of the other virgins" (Esther 2:17). Was there a purpose behind this favor? Certainly. The favor that rested upon her eventually made her queen, and as queen she came to the place where her true colors would shine. Mordecai brought word to her that her own Jewish people would be destroyed if she didn't act. Esther 4:13-14 states, "Do not think that because you are in the king's house you alone of all the Jews will escape. For if you remain silent at this time, relief and deliverance for the Jews will arise from another place, but you and your father's family will perish. *And who knows but that you have come to royal position for such a time as this?*" (emphasis added)

Who knows what God can do through you? How do you know that you are not here for a time such as this? God designed and knew the hour and minute you would be born. You are the one He needs. Will you let Him use you? Moses, even though he felt totally unequipped, was a yielded vessel. He felt so unworthy of his calling that he even said, "Oh Lord, please send someone else to do it." Yet because of his obedience the Israelites were led out from under Pharaoh's rule. Nehemiah helped rebuild the wall of Jerusalem. Daniel, after being rescued from the lion's den, watched as King Darius made a decree that all the people were to fear and reverence his God. The list goes on and on as the Bible is strewn with examples of individual lives that made lasting impressions in history.

Inside each and everyone one of us there is a purpose and a role to play in the Kingdom of God. And if one yielded vessel can make such a difference, then imagine what one yielded church can do. The church is the people, not a building. It is comprised of people who should be moving in the same direction with the same vision with the same heart. Can you imagine what it could be like if each individual in the church came together and yielded themselves as a whole unit to the leadership of their pastor who in turn was yielded to the leading of the Holy Spirit? You would have a church that was unstoppable, a church that throbbed with the heartbeat of God.

Our Last Time Together

In November 1996, Thanksgiving weekend, our entire family was together for the first time in years. My sister, 40 years old at the time, who had been trying to have a baby, came with the great news of her pregnancy. It was also the same weekend that my dad heard me preach my first sermon. It was a weekend that we all will remember as the house was filled with joy and excitement.

Following the Thanksgiving holiday celebration, my wife and I prepared to return home. It was Monday and my father drove us to the airport. We chatted about a variety of things on the way, and arriving at the airport I said, "See ya, Dad! I will call you when we get to Florida."

We arrived in Florida late that night, and as the plane landed I promptly called my dad letting him know we had arrived safely. I remember these very words spilling out of my mouth, "Good night, Dad. I will call you later in the week." Little did I know that those words were the last I would speak to my father, and that those moments I had embraced Him at home would be the last time I would receive my father's loving arms.

That next afternoon between noon and one o'clock we received a call that shattered my world. I was told that my father had suddenly passed away. It blew me away. I was shocked, devastated, and numb. A great man of God had been taken off this earth. How could this be? I was sure he had much more to accomplish.

Just a few hours before, I had been with him. He had been there listening to me preach my first sermon. I couldn't conceive in my mind what had just happened. Immediately Kim and I tried to get a flight back home. Unable to fly out that night, we caught a plane the next morning. I remember walking back into the house and seeing the looks on everyone's faces. The entire family was there, just as they had been a few days earlier, but this time everyone's countenances were drastically different. I was the youngest of seven and was the only one who hadn't been there when he had passed away the night before. When I saw my mom, she broke down sobbing.

"DAD, COME BACK"

The whole time I was flying back home I kept pondering the news I had heard. In search of comfort I opened my Bible and began searching the Scriptures. I read about how Jesus, Peter, and Elijah had raised people from the dead. I built up so much faith in God's Word that I began to believe for what seemed like the impossible. The moment I saw my mother, I hugged her and boldly proclaimed, "Mom, I am going down to the funeral home, and I am coming back with Dad." She looked at me like only a mom could do and simply said, "You do what you got to do, son." That was all I needed.

I hopped in the car and drove to the funeral home. When I walked into the parlor, I immediately saw the name, "Thomas Zito" posted outside a room. (My father and I have the same name.) I took off running toward my dad. The director of the funeral home came out, and at first he attempted to stop me but then allowed me to go on. I was on a mission.

I went to the front of the room where I saw my father lying in the casket. And when I saw him, I lost it. I climbed on top of his body, just like Elijah had done, and began to weep and cry out to God for my dad's life. I knew the world needed him and we just couldn't lose this vessel. He was too precious and was making too much of a difference. I yelled, "God...God... God...bring him back, God." I was praying and crying so hard that my tears soaked everything. I was a wreck. It wasn't long before the suit my dad was wearing was totally drenched. It didn't matter to me. I wanted my father back. I went for it and prayed with my whole being. All of a sudden, while I was crying out, the Lord quickened me and I heard these words, "He doesn't want to come back."

ONLY ONE THING THAT MATTERS

In reality, there is no sense in grieving for people who have gone to be with Jesus, because they have stepped over into the glory realm. Our minds cannot conceive it nor understand it because we are finite creatures. It doesn't matter how much my father had loved his family, he wouldn't have returned because he loved his God and his Creator even more. When my father saw Jesus in all His glory and splendor, he had reached home. He had fought the good fight and finished the race.

After hearing God say, "He doesn't want to come back," I slowly removed myself from my father's casket and went to sit down. My whole body felt completely weary and weak from the hours of prayer and all the emotions that were surging through my system. As I was sitting with my head down, I felt what seemed like a hand pushing my head back up. A revelation flooded my being. I walked back over to my father and stood there staring at him. I realized something. The person I was looking at was not my father. His body was there, but my father was gone.

Man has a body, soul, and spirit. What we live in is our earth suit. It enables us to walk in this world. But as Christians, we are not of this world; our home is Heaven. We are spirits. Our real person resides on the inside of us. When life is over, there is only one thing that matters—our relationship with our heavenly Father and where we spend eternity.

Chapter Two

REALIZING
I WAS ASLEEP

Sometimes there are events in life that radically change who we are as a person, and redefine the meaning of our life. This is the story of my testimony that sets my heart's passion for the one and only thing that matters in this world—and that is a person's individual soul. Every day you come face-to-face with someone for whom Jesus died. The question is, do they even know the price that was paid for them? Do they know that eternity awaits them? Do they know there is a Savior? You see, unless someone like you or me tells them, how will they know?

Not What I Had in Mind

My story starts in June of 1995 in New Jersey. I had just completed my first year at Bible school, I was on fire for God and was ready to change the world. I was preparing to marry my lovely wife, Kimberly, and my brother-in-law, Robert, was, helping me land a job, working on a home construction site. I had thoughts of an ordinary job, nice coworkers, a friendly environment, and great teamwork. Boy, was I mistaken. Once I parked my car near the worksite, any ideas about an easy job quickly subsided.

The very first day I arrived at the construction site, I realized there was no way possible that I was going to drive my little car through that site. Attempting that move would have been like playing ping-pong with massive rocks, resulting in a demolished sports car. The thing to do was leave the car outside the site and jump into a large 4 x 4 truck with all your construction worker buddies. (Actually, "buddies" was not the word. How many of you know what construction workers are really like? Well, in New York, you don't want to mess with construction workers. My best and only description would be big boots, jeans, muscles the size of bowling balls, tattoos all over, and long pony tails. You just don't want to mess with them. Yes, it's a stereotype, I know; but it's my story.)

They had no idea when I stepped out of the car on that first morning at around 6:15 that they would be confronted with a young man planning on a career in the ministry. Regardless, they found it necessary to circle around and look me over. I even got a few laughs and chuckles. I stood out like a sore thumb. I was the Italian kid who obviously didn't belong, because I wasn't chugging down a beer like the rest of them. But before I knew it, the circle had diminished, and they all jumped in their trucks leaving me to fend for myself. Talk about feeling a moment of rejection. I thought, *Oh my goodness, what am I going to do?*

Surprisingly, this guy came out from around the corner, walked up to me, and said, "Tommie, you know you don't have to listen to those guys." The young man in his mid-twenties with long straggly hair, red eyes, most likely because he was hooked on something, continued, "Tommie, your brother-in-law, Robert, told me to take care of you. My name is Frankie." Even his name brought relief, being Italian and everything! He said, "You can come with me in my truck, and I'll take you down to the construction site." I was praising God because the site was at least a mile away. Without hesitating, I jumped in his truck.

At the exact moment I stepped foot into his truck, God did something to me. He tugged on my heart so strongly I will never forget it. I am sure you remember instances where God has done this to you. It comes upon you so strongly when you come in contact with someone who doesn't know Jesus. The tug on my heart begged, "Tell him about Me, tell him about Me, tell him about Me, Tommie. Tell him about Me. He needs you to tell him about Me." I quickly responded, "Hold on, Lord. Time out! I just got a ride. You want me to tell this guy about You? All he has to say is, 'Get out of here.' Then I'll be walking."

I MISSED WHAT MATTERED MOST

Now let's recap some things. I had just completed my first year of Bible school, and I was on fire for God—supposedly...*supposedly*. And out of nowhere, God challenged me. And how did I react? I said, "No, no, no, Lord. I can't tell him. Just give me some time. Let me get to know him a little bit. I'm a cool guy. I'm Italian. Once I get to know him a little bit, I will come at him from the backside with the gospel. Then he will get saved."

Everyone knows that line, and I am sure many have used it. We often try to make this deal with God about how we think it should happen. We rest in the fact that we will tell them when we feel the time is right. But many times, we often fail at even opening our mouths to share the truth. Sadly, I let that one opportune moment slip by. How did I know that he didn't wake up one of those mornings saying, "Lord, reveal Yourself to me. Make Yourself real to me. Let me know that You care about me"? And all the while the Lord was impressing on me to tell him.

Frankie never did get to hear. Every day I jumped into Frankie's truck as he drove me to the construction site, and every single day he drove me back home. I built a great rapport with him. Every day as we rode to work we made time to talk about how bad the day was going to be, and every day on our drive home we talked about how bad the boss was. We made time to talk about everything except what mattered most. As soon as Frankie would drop me off at the end of the workday, I would race to my car, yelling out "See ya, Frankie," and jet home to go to a service that night. Remember, I was on fire for God! I was in revival! I made sure I got to that revival service and right on time. I was not going to miss that for the world.

WE HAVE TO WAKE UP FRANKIE!

Two months following the day I first stepped on the construction site, I boldly asked for time off to get prepared for my upcoming wedding. It was a Wednesday and I was given the next two days off. Getting a few days off was the highlight of my week, so I made sure I rubbed it into Frankie that Wednesday after work. "Ah, get out of here," he said. We had that kind of relationship. I yelled back, "Hey I'll catch you on Monday, man." On Thursday, I ran to pick up my tuxedo, set up my flight plans, and make other wedding arrangements. Friday morning, as I was preparing to work on some additional wedding plans, the doorbell rang. It was around eleven or twelve o'clock. I opened the door to find my brother-in-law, Robert, standing there with a shocked look on his face.

Now, seeing Robert that morning was weird because he was supposed to be working at another location of that same home construction site. I said, "Robert, what are you doing here? I'm off today, remember?" He said, "Tommie, work was cancelled today." I said, "Work was cancelled today? Yeah right, I take off work and they decide to cancel it. Ya know, that's how it goes." I was in my own world. I had not awakened yet. Then I saw something in his face. He said, "No, you don't understand."

"Do you know Frankie?" I said, "Yes, of course, what do you mean? If there is anybody I know, it's Frankie. Yeah, yeah, I know him. Why?" He said, "Ah...well...Frankie didn't show up for work this morning."

Now, Frankie had never missed a day of work. Robert then began telling me the scenario that had taken place earlier that morning. Since it was so out of the ordinary for Frankie to miss a day, and since they had already tried to call to wake him up only to receive no answer, they decided to go and motivate him to get to work.

That day they happened to be shorthanded and were in dire need of help. Frankie lived only five minutes from the housing site so Robert said, "Let's go get this guy out of bed. He's probably still sleeping from partying all night. We need to get him back to work." Shortly after, Robert and a few construction guys pulled up in the driveway, and parked there was the same 4 x 4 blue truck that took me to work. Slowly they approached the house and rang the doorbell, only to have no one come to unlock and answer the door.

When they first arrived, they had heard loud rock-and-roll music, and it became apparent that Frankie was still there. So they said, "Let's go around back." Knocking on the back door, they got the same results—nothing, no answer, no response. It was strange. He hadn't showed up for work; he hadn't called in; he wasn't answering his phone; and his truck was in the drive-way. Something was not right. Something was strange. So the only option left was to break into the house. Once inside, with music blaring, the search began through the house and to a slightly opened bathroom door. Hesitantly approaching, they pushed the bathroom door until it was fully open. There lying on the floor was Frankie. He had committed suicide. His body was filled with 25 times the amount of heroin that would normally kill a human being.

TODAY IS THE DAY OF SALVATION

Listen to me carefully, Church. I will never forget what I was wearing the day my brother-in-law told me the news. As soon as the words reverberated in my head that Frankie was dead, the power of God fell on me so strong, like never before in a service. I heard these words audibly, "Today is the day of sal-vation—today." I heard God say it. His voice pierced my heart, and the power of God came on me. And all I could do was weep and tremble.

I was on fire for God. I was going to be a great healing evan-gelist. "Come, come, bring the sick. Bring the blind here." I was going to be a great man of God and pack the stadiums out. I would say, "Lord, Lord, use me, Lord"...and there was Frankie. "Pastor, give me the service"...and there was Frankie. I was always in a hurry rushing to my car to make it to meeting after meeting after meeting. I ran to revival service after revival service after revival service.

At the funeral we discovered that distant relatives had been praying for that man forever. And guess what? Here was the answer to prayer—I just completed my first year of Bible school. "Use me, Lord." And He had said, "Okay. You want to be used? Okay, here is the situation." "But wait. Wait, Lord. That is not what I had envisioned."

Last-minute miracles don't happen all the time. Heaven and hell are real places. But we don't preach much about hell, and we don't tell people they are going to hell. Hell is a real place. Frankie was on that road, and I was sitting back saying, "Lord, move. Lord, do something." The Lord said, "You move, you tell him." And Frankie, needing a last-minute miracle, will now spend eternity in hell.

Do you know how long an eternity is? Think about as far as you can think, and then keep thinking. Then think about as far as you can think and then keep thinking. Hell will never end. Our finite minds can't comprehend it. We see everything with a finish and an end. This Christian walk that we walk is not a game. People's eternal destinies are at stake forever. I didn't have to get Frankie saved. That wasn't my job. I couldn't save Frankie. My job was to give him an opportunity to know the Savior. That was my job, and I failed.

GOD SAYS, "DO SOMETHING— TELL THEM ABOUT ME"

I will never fail again. I will never let it happen again. I will never let someone who doesn't know Jesus Christ come into my sphere and my life without giving them an opportunity to know Him. I didn't even give Frankie an opportunity.

I was on fire for God...supposedly. But what does it mean to be on fire for God? Is it coming to a meeting and running around and falling down? If it is that, then I did it all the time. No, when someone is on fire for God, they tell people about

Jesus. I will show you someone on fire for God when I show you someone hanging out with sinners and sharing the love of Jesus with them.

When life is over, only one thing matters—either a person goes up or down. A great man of God had a vision that I will never forget in regard to souls. He was standing on a road and the road forked two ways. Multitudes, like an army, were going down one road, while a handful was going down the other road. He himself was fixed in the middle of the fork in the road and watched as people slowly passed by him on both sides.

The multitudes walked toward what was a cliff, while the small handful went up to a beautiful mountain and a beautiful place. When those in the multitudes got to the cliff, you could see fire and smoke coming out from the edge of the place they were going. And as they followed each other to the cliff, not really paying attention, they began to fall, one after another. It looked like Niagara Falls. What he was actually seeing were people falling into the pit of hell. The sound was indescribable and horrific. No horror movie could depict it. It was terrifying.

The man screamed out to God, "How could You let this happen? Why don't You do something?" That is the cry of most Christians today, "God, why don't You do something?" God's answer to this man was interesting: "Why don't you?"

Frankie was on the same road those multitudes were on. He was following the crowd and doing what everybody else was doing. He didn't know any better. But God had put me between Frankie and the cliff and said, "Tell him about Me. I already went over the cliff for Him. He doesn't have to go. I have made a way, the other road, the road to life." He puts the church, every day, in the paths of people who are on their way to the cliff, and says, "Tell them about Me." That is why we go to church, so we can make a difference for people on the way to the cliff. We are not waiting on God; He is waiting on us.

There are people all over the place on that same road. They are all over America, and all over the world. It is up to you and me as Christ's ambassadors to open our mouths with the divine truth. Never let another Frankie walk into and out of your life without introducing them to HIM!

Chapter Three

HEAVEN OR HELL

We live in a complex world where thousands of messages are transmitted to our minds each day. People with erroneous ideas seek to control us and continually attempt to persuade us to accept their false concepts of life. The key is to know who you are and what you believe. You may believe that there are no consequences for sin or you may believe that God in His infinite mercy will save everyone. I've heard of one prominent preacher who is so deceived to believe that everyone in the world is already saved. In stating and believing this, he is actually saying that you can go ahead and live like the devil. If it feels good, do it, because we all are going to heaven—a message that essentially gives you a license to sin. Jesus did not shed His blood so we could have permission to sin. He shed His blood to save us from the consequences of our sin.

HELL IS REAL

In the Book of Luke, we find a man who had all his needs met and consequently lived a life of complete pleasure. Thinking and caring only for himself, he left absolutely no room for others. In his selfishness, he disregarded the needs of those around him.

> *There was a certain rich man, which was clothed in purple and fine linen, and fared sumptuously every day: and there was a certain beggar named Lazarus, which was laid at his gate, full of sores, and desiring to be fed with the crumbs*

which fell from the rich man's table: moreover the dogs come and licked his sores. And it came to pass, that the beggar died, and was carried by the angels into Abraham's bosom: the rich man also died, and was buried; and in hell he lift up his eyes, being in torments, and seeth Abraham afar off, and Lazarus in his bosom. And he cried and said, Father Abraham, have mercy on me, and send Lazarus, that he may dip the tip of his finger in water, and cool my tongue; for I am tormented in this flame. But Abraham said, Son, remember that thou in thy lifetime receivedst thy good things, and likewise Lazarus evil things: but now he is comforted, and thou art tormented. And beside all this, between us and you there is a great gulf fixed: so that they which would pass from hence to you cannot; neither can they pass to us, that would come from thence. Then he said, I pray thee therefore, father, that thou wouldest send him to my father's house: for I have five brethren; that he may testify unto them, lest they also come into this place of torment. Abraham saith unto him, They have Moses and the prophets; let them hear them. And he said, Nay, father Abraham: but if one went unto them from the dead, they will repent. And he said unto him, If they hear not Moses and the prophets, neither will they be persuaded, though one rose from the dead (Luke 16:19-31 KJV).

This man, who seemingly had everything the world had to offer, found himself in the very grips of hell. The Scriptures tell us that while on earth, he fared sumptuously every day. He made sure that his natural needs were met but had no concern for his spiritual condition. Whether he believed in hell or not, he was now experiencing it.

NOT HELL, BUT A SAVIOR, WAS CREATED FOR MANKIND

Hell is not a figment of the imagination. It is a real place. However, hell wasn't originally made so that God would have a consequence for people who did bad things. It was never created for people or mankind. Hell was made for the enemy. Mankind was made to fellowship with and worship God Almighty. Man was made to walk with God in the cool of the day and to have a relationship with Him. It was through man's choices that the fellowship with God Almighty was broken. Mankind fell and sin nature came. Because of that sin nature, man needed a Savior.

Knowing the need for a Savior, God sent His only begotten Son to die and pay the price for all mankind. It would be those who believe in Him and who receive Him as the sacrificial Lamb, who would be reconnected with the Father. They would not have to pay the price for their sins, because God's Son had already paid the price. God took the very nature of sin on Himself on the cross—every sin and sick thing was laid upon Jesus.

While hanging on the cross, at the height of all that was taking place, Jesus said, "My God, My God, why have You forsaken Me?" (Mk. 15:34) The sight was too much to bear. The Word tells us that God Himself had to turn His back on His only begotten Son. While nailed to the cross, He paid for every mistake that was made. No one man or one group is responsible for killing Jesus—not the Jews, not the Romans soldiers, not the religious Pharisees. All in all, it was our sin that killed Jesus. It was our mess-ups and our mistakes. But thank God, in His infinite grace and mercy, He sent His Son on our behalf. Yes, Jesus died, but God raised Him up. He was the sinless, spotless Lamb of God, slain before the foundation of the world.

Nevertheless, following the crucifixion and resurrection of Jesus Christ, hell still exists, and those who refuse to receive the sacrifice of Jesus for their own sins choose their own destination. People who do not allow Jesus to take the place of their sins ultimately choose a route that means they themselves will be paying the consequences for their own sin. The so very sad and unnecessary reality is that they don't have to. It was never intended that anyone go to hell. It was never created for them. Nonetheless they choose their own way. They *choose*. Hello! Don't let anyone ever tell you that sin was forced upon them, or that they were born "that way." The Bible says everyone chooses sin. People feel safe being able to say they were born a certain way because it transfers the responsibility from themselves to something or someone else. We are not born certain ways and then sent to hell having no control of our own choices or our own destiny. God is a just God. We choose our own destination.

PHYSICAL AND MENTAL SUFFERING IN HELL

"And in hell he lift up his eyes...." Do you know that in hell you can see? The rich man saw Abraham and Lazarus. This man lifted up his eyes in hell. Hell is much worse than simply burning. Hell is eternal torment. In hell, people will recognize and see!

"And he cried and said...." You will have a voice in hell. You will hear. You will be able to talk and communicate. You won't just shrivel into ashes. You will thirst. You will be able to feel and touch. You will have the same physical abilities and senses that you had on earth.

"But Abraham said, Son, remember...." In hell, you will have mental abilities. You will be able to remember in hell. Your memory will not be burned up. You will be aware of your past life, your past decisions and choices. You will remember your life as it was lived on earth.

Hell is not the end of life. You won't just burn up and die and be no more. You will be able to see, recognize, hear, speak, feel, and above all, remember. These facts are what make hell so tormenting. I believe you will be able to see what could have been. People will realize that they have no fellowship with God, and suddenly, they will want to be with their Creator. The realization that they missed eternal life with God will grip them and make life in hell unbearable.

SEND SOMEBODY TO WARN THEM

Then he said, I pray thee therefore, father, that thou wouldest send him to my father's house: for I have five brethren; that he may testify unto them, lest they also come into this place of torment....

You would think those in hell would be very angry and furiously irate that they had gone to such a place, and would react by saying, "I want everybody to burn in hell!" You would expect an angry resentful disposition—"If I am here, I want everybody else to be here." But we find an entirely different attitude.

Hell is so torturous and tormenting, a place of continuous weeping and gnashing of teeth, where people are consumed by flames, that you wouldn't wish it on your worst enemy. You will pray like the rich man—that your family never has to come to such a place.

"Can you send people to go testify and witness so that they don't have to come here?"

This man in hell had more passion to win souls than people who were living on the earth. Why? He finally realized what life is all about.

PAID IN FULL

Those who believe you turn into a grasshopper or a fish when you die are under some major form of deception. When it is all over, you won't turn into a tree. You won't float like a cloud or swim in the sea. There are consequences for the way we live our life here on earth. God puts the responsibility in your hands. It is a consequence that determines whether you go up or down. The choice is yours. Realize always that God in His great mercy already sent His Son in our place. He went down for us. He went down into hell, into this place of torment, and took our place. He paid the price for our sin. When people choose to go to hell, they are unnecessarily paying the price for something that has been already been paid for.

While Jesus was on the cross, He said the most profound and impacting words during His final hours. Just before He died, He gathered all His strength and exclaimed, "Teleytha," a word that means, "It is finished." "Teleytha" was a word used in Bible times that meant the debt was paid in full. Everything was paid in full. When Jesus said, "It is finished," He was saying, "It is paid in full." He paid the price for all of us.

TO RECEIVE OR NOT RECEIVE
WHAT WE DESERVE

The Word tells us that "it is appointed unto men once to die, but after this, the judgment (Heb. 9:27 KJV). Two things are for sure—no matter how much faith you have to believe otherwise, you will not live forever on this earth, and you will face judgment. We are told in God's Word that everybody will give an account for his or her works. Every single person who has ever lived will one day stand trial at the Great White Throne Judgment. This world is the only hell that Christians will ever know, and this world is also the only heaven that others will ever know. Men and women will face their sin and realize they are receiving what they deserve but what could have been avoided because the price has already been paid.

Get a reality of hell. As you live your daily life, consider that there is a hell that people step into every day. Open the newspaper and read the obituaries. I just wonder...as Christians who are forgiven and touched by God's grace and love, how important is it that we share this message with others? Hell is a real place, and people really go there.

HEAVEN

I John, who also am your brother, and companion in tribulation, and in the kingdom and patience of Jesus Christ, was in the isle that is called Patmos, for the word of God, and for the testimony of Jesus Christ. I was in the Spirit on the Lord's day, and heard behind me a great voice, as of a trumpet, saying, I am Alpha and Omega, the first and the last: and, What thou seest, write in a book, and send it unto the seven churches which are in Asia; unto Ephesus, and unto Smyrna, and unto Pergamos, and unto Thyatira, and unto Sardis, and unto Philadelphia, and unto Laodicea. And I turned to see the voice that spake with me. And being turned, I saw seven golden candlesticks; and in the midst of the seven candlesticks one like unto the Son of man, clothed with a garment down to the foot, and girt about the paps with a golden girdle. His head and His hairs were white like wool, as white as snow; and His eyes were as a flame of fire; and His feet like unto fine brass, as if they burned in a furnace; and His voice as the sound of many waters. And He had in his right hand seven stars: and out of His mouth went a sharp twoedged sword: and His countenance was as the sun shineth in His strength. And when I saw Him, I fell at His feet as dead... (Rev. 1:9-17 KJV).

And I saw a new heaven and a new earth: for the first heaven and the first earth were passed away; and there was no more sea. And I John saw the holy city, new Jerusalem, coming down from God out of heaven, prepared as a bride adorned for her husband. And I heard a great voice out of heaven saying, Behold, the tabernacle of God is with men, and He will dwell with them, and they shall be His people, and God Himself shall be with them, and be their God. And God shall wipe away all tears from their eyes; and there shall be no more death, neither sorrow, nor crying, neither shall there be any more pain: for the former things are passed away. And He that sat upon the throne said, Behold, I make all things new. And He said unto me, Write: for these words are true and faithful. And He said unto me, It is done. I am Alpha and Omega, the beginning and the end. I will give unto him that is athirst of the fountain of the water of life freely. He that overcometh shall inherit all things; and I will be his God, and he shall be My son....And he carried me away in the spirit to a great and high mountain, and showed me that great city, the holy Jerusalem, descending out of heaven from God, having the glory of God: and her light was like unto a stone most precious, even like a jasper stone, clear as crystal; and had a wall great and high, and had twelve gates, and at the gates twelve angels, and names written thereon, which are the names of the twelve tribes of the children of Israel: on the east three gates; on the north three gates; on the south three gates; and on the west three gates. And the wall of the city had twelve foundations, and in them the names of the twelve apostles of the Lamb. And he that talked with me had a golden reed to measure the city, and the gates thereof, and the wall thereof. And the city lieth foursquare, and the length is as large as the breadth: and he measured the city with the reed, twelve thousand furlongs. The length and the breadth and the height of it are equal. And he measured the wall thereof, an hundred and forty and four cubits, according to the measure of a man, that is, of the angel. And the building of the wall of it was of jasper: and the city was pure gold, like unto clear glass. And the foundations of the wall of the city were garnished with all manner of precious stones. The first foundation was jasper; the second, sapphire; the third, a chalcedony; the fourth, an emerald; the fifth, sardonyx; the sixth, sardius; the seventh, chrysolite; the eighth, beryl; the ninth, a topaz; the tenth, a chrysoprasus; the eleventh, a jacinth; the twelfth, an amethyst. And the twelve gates were twelve pearls; every several gate was of one pearl: and the street of the city was pure gold, as it were transparent glass. And I saw no temple therein: for the Lord God Almighty and the Lamb are the temple of it. And the city had no need of the sun, neither of the moon, to shine in it: for the glory of God did lighten it, and the Lamb is the light thereof. And the nations of them which are saved shall walk in the light of it: and the kings of the earth do bring their glory and honor into it. And the gates of it shall not be shut at all by day: for there shall be no night there. And they shall bring the glory and honor of the nations into it. And there shall in no wise enter into it any thing that defileth, neither whatsoever worketh abomination, or maketh a lie: but they which are written in the Lamb's book of life (Rev. 21:1-7,10-27 KJV).

At the end of life on earth, all that matters is that your name is written down in that book.

And he showed me a pure river of water of life, clear as crystal, proceeding out of the throne of God and of the Lamb. In the midst of the street of it, and on either side of the river, was there the tree of life, which bare twelve manner of fruits, and yielded her fruit every month: and the leaves of the tree were for the healing of the nations. And there shall be no more curse: but the throne of God and of the Lamb shall be in it; and His servants shall serve Him: and they shall see His face; and His name shall be in their foreheads. And there shall be no night there; and they need no candle, neither light of the sun; for the Lord God giveth them light: and they shall reign for ever and ever. And he said unto me, These sayings are faithful and true: and the Lord God of the holy prophets sent His angel to show unto His servants the things which must shortly be done. Behold, I come quickly: blessed is he that keepeth the sayings of the prophecy of this book. And I John saw these things, and heard them. And when I had heard and seen, I fell down to worship before the feet of the angel which showed me these things. Then saith he unto me, See thou do it not: for I am thy fellowservant, and of thy brethren the prophets, and of them which keep the sayings of this book: worship God. And he saith unto me, Seal not the sayings of the prophecy of this book: for the time is at hand. He that is unjust, let him be unjust still: and he which is filthy, let him be filthy still: and he that is righteous, let him be righteous still: and he that is holy, let him be holy still. And, behold, I come quickly; and My reward is with Me, to give every man according as his work shall be. I am Alpha and Omega, the beginning and the end, the first and the last. Blessed are they that do His commandments, that they may have right to the tree of life, and may enter in through the gates into the city. For without are dogs, and sorcerers, and whoremongers, and murderers, and idolaters, and whosoever loveth and maketh a lie. I Jesus have sent Mine angel to testify unto you these things in the churches. I am the root and the offspring of David, and the bright and morning star. And the Spirit and the bride say, Come. And

*let him that heareth say, Come. And let him that is athirst
come. And whosoever will, let him take the water of life
freely. For I testify unto every man that heareth the words
of the prophecy of this book, If any man shall add unto
these things, God shall add unto him the plagues that are
written in this book: and if any man shall take away from
the words of the book of this prophecy, God shall take away
his part out of the book of life, and out of the holy city, and
from the things which are written in this book. He which
testifieth these things saith, Surely I come quickly. Amen.
Even so, come, Lord Jesus. The grace of our Lord Jesus
Christ be with you all. Amen* (Rev. 22:1-21 KJV).

HOLDING UP YOUR END OF THE BARGAIN

Life comes down to one of two places: heaven or hell. You
determine where you will go. The Bible says that multitudes are
in the valley of decision. What are they deciding? They must
make a decision about which way to go, which path to take. The
world says, "Come this way, come with us." And many are traveling that path because they have never been presented with
another way. Only one Man, however, has been able to say, "I am
the way." He didn't say, "Come this way, or go that way." He said,
"I am the way, and the truth, and the life. No one comes to the
Father except through Me" (Jn. 14:6).

And people come to Jesus through you. You are His mouth-
piece. You are the vessel. Through you, the way, the truth, and the
life of Jesus are presented, so that people can make their decision. We are God's hands and feet. We are His body. How you live
your life will determine if others spend forever and ever in
Heaven or hell. Christianity is not just about reading the Bible
and listening to a good sermon on Sunday. My question to you
is: Are you holding up your end of the bargain?

When you received Him as Savior, He took all your sins,
mistakes, and shortcomings. And you made an exchange. You
said, "Lord, I give you my life. I will go. I'm crucified with You. I

give You everything." You became born again. You became a new creature. Old things have passed away, behold all are new.

Are you holding up your end of the bargain? Are you doing for Him what He did for you? Did you mean what you said when you gave Him your life? Keeping your promise to live for Him determines if people spend their eternity in heaven or hell. It is about your obedience. God doesn't ask us to get others saved. That's impossible. Neither have we been instructed to manipulate, motivate, or convince others. The gospel is not to be debated. It is to be preached, proclaimed, and presented. Be God's messenger. Tell others about the exchange, that they too can exchange all their shortcomings and mistakes for His righteousness.

People in both heaven and hell want to send messengers. God is waiting for messengers. The world is waiting for messengers.

Chapter Four

YOU HAVE BEEN ASLEEP

For change to occur in a person's life, he or she must first recognize his or her unsatisfactory present condition or state, and then determine the desirable state or condition they would like to be in. An alcoholic has to recognize that he is an alcoholic before he can overcome his behavior. A perfectionist must recognize that he has a problem before he can break his perfectionism. Someone with a temper must recognize his difficulty with handling anger before he can learn to control it. So it is with the narcoleptic. Someone who is often in a deep sleep must recognize that he has a problem with sleeping before he can be awakened.

A DISENGAGED MIND

Have you ever been sitting in a classroom fully focused on your instructor and the lesson, and then disappointingly discover you have somehow drifted off into another world? Maybe you can recall a time you were cramming for a major exam, or pulling an all-nighter with every intent on staying awake. You didn't think you were tired at the time. Then, without recognizing it, you fell asleep only to wake up hours later, totally unprepared for the exam?

Perhaps you are one of those people who prefer to be asleep to help pass the time away, especially when it comes to traveling in a car or plane. I have even heard stories of people falling asleep while talking on the phone, leaving the other person to feel either boring or unimportant. Irregardless of the reason we fall asleep or whether we intend to fall asleep or not, one thing is certain: Sleep completely disengages the mind and brings it to a halt.

Disengaging the mind is a serious thing. You definitely don't want to be disengaged in a moment of urgency when an alert mind is required to function. A good example is driving. It takes a coherent mind aware of its surroundings to drive safely. How about something as simple as being on the job? If your body is there, but your mind is not, you're useless. I have heard of a condition called sleepwalking, which I don't know too much about. In any case, it doesn't sound very safe. The mind must be engaged to be effective. I have concluded that for the most part, we lived in a spiritually disengaged society.

COMATOSE, SLEEPING, OR WIDE-AWAKE

I believe that people fall into one of three categories: a comatose state, sleeping, or wide-awake. Jesus used other terms: cold, lukewarm, and hot.

Those in the comatose state are completely unaware of anything and everything that would affect them or anyone else. The dictionary definition is that of being unconscious, or a lethargic inertness.[2] It comes directly from the word *coma*, which means a deep sleep or unconsciousness caused by an illness or injury. People of this mind-set live haphazardly and presumptuously, without considering imposing dangers. They have no regard for morality, rules, or such. They are tolerant of everything and believe in a society that embraces all. This category consists of those who either believe that there is no God and we are just here by chance, or they believe that God exists, but live with disregard of a heaven or hell reality. Nothing fazes them. They are here for the ride.

Those in the second category are sleeping. Sleep is comfortable, almost too comfortable. When you get to the place of sleep, you get to a place of inertness. You generally do not respond to anything, and if you do, it is usually lashing back at someone who has had the audacity to try to waken up. Sleep is defined as the natural periodic suspension of consciousness.[3] In one sense of the word, it is almost paralyzing. Those things that you do when awake, you cannot do when asleep. It is a basic law of nature.

The sleepers have a tendency to go in and out of their condition. One moment they are awake; the next, snuggled up in a blanket in "happy land." You might call them double minded. One minute they are on fire for the things of God, the next they would rather not even be seen at church. It is almost like a fog or a haze has covered them to where they are blinded to their very own state of being. They want the things of the world, yet desire to have a relationship with Jesus. They enjoy riding the fence and prefer to be gray rather than black or white. Sometimes they take God's grace for granted knowing that He is always there to forgive them. Those who sleep are the ones who find the Word of God relevant and believe in God's truth, but are unaware of applying it to their own lives. They sit in church absorbing the truths but do not really allow the Word of God to sink deep into their hearts.

They are described as the types of soil found in the parable of the sower in Luke chapter 8. As the sower is scattering the seed, some falls along the path, some along the rock, some among the thorns, and others on good soil. Where the Word is sown on the path, people hear it, but the devil comes and takes the Word from their hearts. For those on the rock, no root takes place and in times of testing they fall away. Then, those among the thorns hear the Word but are constantly distracted by life's worries.

Finally, those who are awake and alive to the things of God are similar to the good soil that the seed fell upon. They are those with a genuine heart, and after hearing the Word, retain it and persevere to produce a crop. The Word is so deeply impressed in them that no matter what comes their way, no matter what circumstances they face, no matter what tries to distract them, they steadfastly persist because they have their face fixed on God.

Those who are awake constantly desire more of God in their lives and are doing everything they can to make that possible. They crave Him like a drug or a narcotic. Their desires must be fulfilled. Just as a seriously addicted drug user will kill to get his fix, so should it be with the church—to be high on Him, completely immersed and overflowing with the divine. They impact lives for eternity and flow in the gifts of God. They are so full they overflow onto others. You don't have to wonder if they are believers, because their life speaks for itself. The fruits of the Holy Spirit are clearly evident in their lives. They tell others of the God they serve and lead others to Christ every day. Those who are awake stand out. They realize their God-given potential and His purpose for their lives.

In which category do you find yourself?

Chapter Five

THE WAKE-UP CALL

In Whitefield's sermon, "Marks of a True Conversion," he states:

There are a great many, who bear the name of Christ, that yet do not so much as know what real Christianity is. Hence it is, that if you ask a great many, upon what their hopes of heaven are founded, they will tell you, that they belong to this, or that, or the other denomination, and part of Christians, into which Christendom is happily divided. If you ask others, upon what foundation they have built their hope of heaven, they will tell you, that they have been baptized, that their fathers and mothers, presented them to the Lord Jesus Christ in their infancy; and though, instead of fighting under Christ's banner, they have been fighting against him, almost ever since they were baptized, yet because they have been admitted to the church, and their names are in the Register book of the parish, there fore they will make us believe, that their names are also written in the book of life. But a great many, who will not build their hopes of salvation upon such a sorry rotten foundation as this, yet if they are, what we generally call, negatively good people; if they so live as their neighbors cannot say that they do anybody harm, they do not doubt but they shall be happy when they die; nay, I have found many such die, as the scripture speaks, "without any hands in their death." And if a person is what the world calls an honest moral man, if he does justly, and, what the world calls, love a little mercy, is not and then good-natured, reacheth out his hand to the poor, receives the sacrament once or twice a year, and is outwardly sober and honest; the world looks upon such an one as a Christian indeed, and doubtless we are to judge charitably of every such person. There are many likewise, who go on in a round of duties, a model of performances, that think they shall go to heaven; but if you examine them, though they have a CHRIST IN THEIR HEADS, THEY HAVE NO CHRIST IN THEIR HEARTS"[4] (emphasis added).

This deception and ignorance is still evident in our society today. We have not changed. Centuries later this very same condition haunts us. This very same lie exists among people everywhere. Step outside your comfortable house. Take a walk on your lunch break. Spend an hour sharing the gospel with anyone who comes across your path. Your heart will be pierced with the responses you receive when you ask people why they believe they are going to heaven. If you're not affected by their answers, I wonder where you are in your walk with the Savior. As a person who knows the truth, my heart breaks when I hear the reasons people give for believing they are on their way to heaven.

"I am going to heaven because I am a good person"; "I am going to heaven because I attend church"; "I'm going to heaven because I help people." May God deal with our hearts so severely and show us our dire need of Him. We deserve nothing, yet because of His grace and His grace alone are we allowed to dwell with Him forever. It is on no merit of our own. May we be stripped of these lies that entrap. May we not be victims of ignorance.

ARE YOU IGNORING THE WAKE-UP CALL?

To ignore is a choice. To ignore is simply to pay no attention to or even to reject. The question I lay before you now is: Are you ignoring the wake-up call? Are you rejecting the call to rise up out of the current state you are in? I'm alarmed by the thought that anyone would choose to disregard a warning or a wake-up call. If someone were to approach me, warning of a certain disaster, I would not be comfortably sitting back waiting for it to happen. I would do everything needed to prepare for my safety and well-being, whether that would be through my heart's condition or my actions.

BUILDING A WAKE-UP CALL

In the Book of Genesis, chapter 7, we read about a situation where individuals chose to ignore what was transpiring right before their very eyes. In the days of Noah, wickedness prevailed. Every imagination of man's heart was evil. God's original plan for mankind was to have relationship with him, not to contend with him. Therefore, seeing the condition of man grieved the heart of God even to the point of being filled with pain. Yet in the midst of this, one man grabbed the attention of God, and his name was Noah.

Noah was a man who stood out among the rest. He was a man with whom God's favor rested. In the middle of a land that had lost sight of its Creator, Noah walked with God. He was found to be righteous and blameless. Noah did not compromise one bit, and it is because of Noah that we as humans still exist to this day. Had he not been following diligently after the Lord, he and his family would not have been spared. God confided in Noah and proceeded to tell him of His plan to put an end to all people because of the violence and wickedness that had filled the entire earth. He gave Noah specific plans to build an ark that would later spare him, his family, and the creatures of the earth.

Now you would think, that in the middle of this land, an ark being designed and built the size of 300 cubits long, 50 cubits wide, and 30 cubits high would have been very apparent. The subject of the ark would have definitely brought about some interesting conversation and questions. It was probably the talk of the town and the basis of much criticism and mockery. But Matthew 24:37-39 says,

*But as the days of Noah were, so shall also the coming of
the Son of Man be. For as in the days that were before the
flood they were eating and drinking, marrying and giving in
marriage, until the day that Noah entered into the ark, and
knew not until the flood came, and took them all away; so
shall also the coming of the Son of man be* (KJV).

While people gave way to their selfish ambitions and worldly
way of living, Noah obediently prepared an ark. God doesn't call
us to succeed, but to obey. Later his obedience would prove faithful as every living thing on the face of the earth was wiped out
except for the people and creatures on the ark. You would think as
people saw Noah and his family preparing the ark, they would
have questioned the meaning of it, and would have done everything possible to find a way to be found blameless in the sight of
the Lord. Sadly, we see no sign of that in Genesis.

BARGAINING A WAKE-UP CALL

A few chapters later we find that although the earth had
been replenished, wickedness had once again found a way to corrupt. In Genesis 18, God confided to Abraham His plans:

*"Shall I hide from Abraham what I am about to do? Abra-
ham will surely become a great and powerful nation, and all
nations on earth will be blessed through him. For I have chosen him, so that he will direct his children and his household
after him to keep the way of the Lord by doing what is right
and just, so that the Lord will bring about for Abraham
what he has promised him." Then the Lord said, "The outcry
against Sodom and Gomorrah is so great and their sin so
grievous that I will go down and see if what they have done
is as bad as the outcry that has reached Me. If not, I will
know"* (Gen. 18:17-21).

In the next verses Abraham pleaded for the city of Sodom.
Abraham cried out that if there were 50 righteous people in the
city, of God would be willing to spare it. The discussion regarding the number of righteous people went back and forth so that
the Lord eventually promised that if there be even 10 righteous

people left in the city, it would be spared. We all know the story. Sodom and Gomorrah, entangled in sin, became no more. Did Abraham's nephew, Lot, heed the warning? Yes, he and his daughters heeded the wake-up call and ran from the city. But those who chose unrighteousness were destroyed.

WAKE-UP CALL AFTER WAKE-UP CALL

This continual cycle exists in the Scriptures where there are clear and distinct lines between good and evil. Throughout God's Word you can find instance after instance where God desired to pull His creation to Himself, yet people chose to run to other idols and gods. This was far from what God ever planned or intended. In the Book of Judges, the cycle is repeated over and over. The Israelites chose to do evil in the eyes of the Lord, forgetting their God. Time after time, God sent a judge to draw them back to Himself—judges like Deborah, Gideon, Samson, and others. In the midst of God's continual faithfulness, Israel lost sight of its first love. But wake-up calls kept sounding...and sounding...and sounding.

The calls sound through the Books of the major and minor prophets, such as Isaiah, Jeremiah, Lamentations, Ezekiel, Daniel, Hosea, Joel, Amos, Obadiah, Jonah, Micah, Nahum, Habakkuk, Zephaniah, Haggai, Zechariah, and Malachi. God continually warned His people of their wickedness, and longed to draw them back to Himself. In Joel 2:12, God's love is clearly evident as He says,

> *"Even now," declares the Lord, "return to Me with all your heart, with fasting and weeping and mourning." Rend your heart and not your garments. Return to the Lord your God, for He is gracious and compassionate, slow to anger and abounding in love, and He relents from sending calamity.*

Joel, the prophet was assigned to warn the people of an upcoming disaster. Were the people told? Yes. Were they alerted or concerned? No. They were in sleep mode, totally unaware and unconcerned with the activity around them. The result was inevitable…with no one preparing for protection or heeding the "call," the Assyrians attacked.

SEPTEMBER 11, 2001

Let's now consider a wake-up call that has recently been sounded and is much closer to home.

It was an event that shook people as they watched in horror as the two World Trade Centers in New York City fell to the earth with a crashing blow. It is not something that can be described with words, nor is it something that viewers will ever forget. Our lives will never be the same.

When these specific incidents occurred, God revealed something to my heart. In 1999, I had been asked to be the director of a large crusade called "Good News New York." For six weeks, Pastor Rodney Howard-Browne set a "mandate" to gather as many churches together and people to spread the gospel to every person they could find in the city and to tell them the Good News. We were given permission to use Madison Square Garden as the center point. In six weeks' time, people branched throughout the city going into every nook and cranny to tell others about Jesus. The World Trade Center was no exception. People were saved outside, inside, and even under the World Trade Center. We serve an all-knowing God; and before anything happens, good or bad, God knows it. I believe He sent us, two years before the horrific events of September 11, because He cares about eternal destinies. While in New York that summer, I witnessed over 49,000 people give their hearts to Christ.

My question again to you is this: Are you ignoring the wake-up calls? They are everywhere. Can't you hear them? God is drawing you closer to Him, away from a place of stagnancy, away from a place of sleep. Awaken yourselves. He has appointed you for a task. He is inviting you to become part of His great army!

Chapter Six

RECOGNIZING RELIGION

Before I stepped into full-time ministry, and before I allowed God to really grip my heart, I first had to realize that I was religious.

I had spent the majority of my life in church. There were times when I halfheartedly walked through Christianity and did some things that I am ashamed of, but I never really strayed from church as a whole. In fact, I was in church every week, reading my Bible and convening with the Lord. I never needed deliverance from a sinful life of drugs and alcohol. Blatant backsliding against God was an area I did not touch. There was that one area, though, that caught me completely off guard, and it was the area of religion.

I was what you would call "religious," and what I needed was freedom. Frankie's life showed that clearly. Most often, the ones who think they could never be religious are the ones who are. None of us have "arrived." There are some people with titles who want other people to think they have all the answers to the Bible...and they are sitting in dangerous territory.

None of us have finally learned everything there is to know. Often, we as humans make the mistake of thinking that our finite minds can understand all His ways, but that is impossible. First Corinthians 1:25 says, "For the foolishness of God is wiser than man's wisdom, and the weakness of God is stronger than man's strength." Isaiah 55:8-9 states, " 'For My thoughts are not your thoughts, neither are your ways My ways,' declares the Lord. As the heavens are higher than the earth, so are My ways higher than your ways and My thoughts than your thoughts."

We serve such a mighty and magnificent God that our minds cannot even fathom all of who He is or His greatness. We probably know about one millionth of God, if even that. Jesus did say that if we have seen Him, we have seen the Father. But He gave us only a portion. Although we should always be growing and learning, He knew we would never be capable of understanding all of God's ways. The Bible says if all the things Jesus did were written, the books of the world would not be able to contain them. He gave us only what we would need to know for the present time. The first sign of being religious is thinking we know and understand all. And isn't that what the Pharisees thought?

MERCY, NOT RELIGION

In Matthew 9:12-13, after the Pharisees asked the disciples why Jesus was eating with sinners, Jesus responded, "They that be whole need not a physician, but they that are sick. But go ye and learn what that meaneth, I will have mercy, and not sacrifice: for I am not come to call the righteous, but sinners to repentance" (KJV). The Message Bible puts it this way:

> Later when Jesus was eating supper at Matthew's house with His close followers, a lot of disreputable characters came and joined them. When the Pharisees saw Him keeping this kind of company, they had a fit, and lit into Jesus' followers. "What kind of example is this from your Teacher, acting cozy with crooks and riff-raff?" Jesus overhearing shot back, "Who needs a doctor: the healthy or the sick? Go figure out what this Scripture means: 'I'm after mercy, not religion.' I'm here to invite outsiders, not coddle insiders."

Wow. That is Jesus for you—so profound, always doing things that surprise, yet cause us to think.

Jesus is after mercy. His heart is to save the sinner. He hit the nail on the head comparing the sinner to the sick needing a doctor. God is the ultimate physician. Again He states, "I'm here to invite outsiders, not coddle insiders." Are we inviting the outsiders or are we shunning them? Do we pay more attention to the so-called "insider" than the ones who are lost? The Pharisees carried with them a feeling of "holier than thou." They knew they were right and were determined to prove everyone else wrong. They left no room in their hearts for the possibility that they themselves could be mistaken. Being utterly deceived and blind, they missed what it was all about. When it comes to the sinner, God's grace and mercy abound.

As a Christian, never allow yourself to become so deceived that you think you are better than someone else. Know that you are who you are because of Christ, and that others need the same Christ to change their lives around. The only difference between me and you, and the homeless man, the prostitute, or the crooked businessman is Jesus. Pray that you walk as Jesus walked, see as He saw, and touch as He touched.

What I Saw Changed My Life

It was in February 1998 when I was on the road, traveling as an assistant to my pastor, Dr. Rodney Howard-Browne. In Ozark, Alabama, he had been given a dream from heaven to launch one of the biggest soul-winning events in the history of New York City. That year, my wife and I were sent to New York City, which just happened to be the area where I grew up, to prepare a year and a half for the crusade. We took on the task of inviting the 34,000-plus churches in NYC to be a part of the crusade. We mailed many letters, made countless phone calls, and scheduled numerous lunches and group meetings with pastors. What I saw changed my life and future ministry forever.

Every evening I would go home and either cry or get sick to my stomach, literally, over the spiritual diarrhea that I saw operating within these so-called leaders. We called them the "gatekeepers"—pastors who formed coalitions to keep "wolves" from entering the gates of their city. The spiritual foundation for what they did was almost non-existent. When sitting down with these men, seldom did I feel they loved Jesus with their whole being. It was as if I was meeting with a bunch of religious Pharisees. Seldom did they show any excitement about going out to win lost souls. Hearts were hardened. Many had become either cold, or burned by the political system of the church, and they carried the attitude of "been there, done that." To them, we were just another somebody trying to be the "savior" of their city and solve all their problems. As a young man, I expected to see leaders full of fire, with desperation for the many souls who surrounded them on their very own streets. But...nothing. In fact, I can't remember seeing one of them witness or share his faith with one soul in a restaurant, coffee shop, or anywhere.

I understand that God has given the fivefold ministry for the equipping of the saints for the work of the ministry. And if these pastors had been equipping their sheep with what they themselves were expressing, then I could truly understand why NYC was in the shape that it was. I was aghast at the things I saw and heard. Some pastors were found doing everything from stealing to using profanity. One pastor walked into my office, pointed at the wall, and said, "I am not working with you if he is" (pointing to a name listed on the wall of another pastor who ministered right down the street from him). "Get rid of him." Another well-known leader of a large church telephoned me and told me that because he saw my pastor associating with another minister, he had to regretfully decline to work with us. One leader stood across the table from me and said, "We don't believe in evangelism." (That's one I've never seen in the Bible.) Another well-known street minister sat across from us and asked, "Instead of spending money to rent Madison Square Garden, could you give it to me for my new building?"

There were so many pastors we met who would constantly tell us why they couldn't get involved or why a revival couldn't take place. Encouragement was hard to come by. Faith was scarce. Please understand that I am not degrading all pastors or churches. In New York City, there are pastors with whom we are still very close to today and who walked me through some situations as a young minister; and our ministry cries out daily for men of God like those around America.

I love New York City. I believe it was by divine ordinance that I was chosen to help direct the New York City crusade at age 24, and someday our team will go back and stay for an extended season. I realized that the Lord would allow me to see certain things even as He allowed Ezekiel to see the dry bones come to life again. I was placed in situations that only God could have ordained. He wanted to show me why the city was in the shape it was, and my life will forever be changed by what I saw that year. It comes down to being directly related to its spiritual leaders. I saw a sleeping church busy with everything but the harvest. There are so many city coalitions and pastor alliances yet still no passion and hunger for the Kingdom. It's the most political institution I have ever seen. If the church ever wakes up, millions will be saved—millions.

Since that time in New York, my heart has become burdened for our nation of America, a nation that was built on godly principles and founded on truth. We are a nation desperately longing to be ushered into an awakening that strips us of all unrighteous ways until we are solely focused on the Almighty God.

GOING THROUGH THE MOTIONS

During the awakening that took place in 1740-1741, New England's population climaxed at around 300,000. It was out of that 300,000 that approximately 60,000 people gave their hearts to the Lord. And out of that 60,000, an estimated half of those were members of the church.[5] Do you see any similarities in our world today? Many people who get saved in our revivals on the streets are church attendees themselves; and when asked the question of salvation, they don't know the answer. Can you believe that? How can people sit in a church, a house of God, regularly, and not know? What are we preaching?

This basically says to me that while many attend church for the pure sake of growing in the Scriptures and dedicating their lives to God, another great number of them attend primarily for the purpose of fulfilling their "duty," or getting their fill. Jesus warned us about the lukewarm church long ago. I would firmly declare that the churches in America are in the same state today. Even though there might be more people attending church, it is obvious that many are just going through the motions. They know how the church system works and the basic layout of the service. They are in by 10:30, out by 12:00, with a little praise and worship, a time to give, and some preaching in between. We take more time getting ready for the service and making sure we look our best than preparing our hearts. It has gone from the Lord's Day, to the Lord's morning, to the Lord's hour. I have even heard of a 12-minute service held in Florida! What disrespect for God!

HAVING A FORM OF GODLINESS

It is appalling to see how America has drifted so far away from its original biblical foundation. The erosion began slowly, but has accelerated during this 21st century with landmark decisions from the United States Supreme Court. We have ashamedly come to the place where states are contemplating same-sex marriages and advocating sinful behavior that is an abomination in the eyes of a holy and righteous God. Controversies in regard to the moral character and standing of our country are continually being raised.

When praying for America, I heard the Lord speak to me, "The American church cares only what it looks like." It is without substance. It has tried to accommodate the masses, "having a form of godliness but denying the power thereof." In trying to please man instead of God, we have missed it. First Samuel 16:7 says, "The Lord does not look at the things man looks at. Man looks at the outward appearance, but the Lord looks at the heart." It is not about what is seen on the outside that counts; it is something much deeper.

Christians take a stand on the principal of matters in regard to the law, yet they fail to look at where the root of the matter lies. Fighting against same-sex marriages, abortions, stem cell research, and euthanasia has its place; but where are we when that one girl is contemplating having an abortion? Where are we when a person is struggling with the issue of homosexuality? What about that older person who feels hopeless? Do we embrace them? Are we there fighting for them? Are we loving the sinner but hating the sin? We care about the Ten Commandments being removed from the courtroom, but we don't care if people actually break the Ten Commandments. We fight for principle, but not for people. Jesus, however, didn't die for principle; He died for people. And so, before our laws can change, the hearts of our lawmakers must change.

LED BY BLIND MEN

When Jesus talked about the leaven of the Pharisees, He was referring to their hypocrisy. He then proceeded to call them blind guides. Religion can take you nowhere. It is the blind attempting to lead the blind. Jesus repeatedly talked about our eyes: "No man looking back is fit for the Kingdom." "Look up, lift up your eyes." He said the devil has blinded the eyes of many. Hence, we must have a spiritual awakening in our land. We need a fresh perspective. We must have our eyes open and a new way of looking at things, which cannot happen through the eyes of the natural. We walk by faith and not by sight. Leaders themselves must open their spiritual eyes so they can lead the people effectively.

Behold, thou art called a Jew, and restest in the law, and makest thy boast of God, and knowest His will, and approvest the things that are more excellent, being instructed out of the law; and art confident that thou thyself art a guide of the blind, a light of them which are in darkness, an instructor of the foolish, a teacher of babes, which hast the form of knowledge and of the truth in the law. Thou therefore which teachest another, teachest thou not thyself? Thou that preachest a man should not steal,

*dost thou steal? Thou that sayest a man should not commit
adultery, dost thou commit adultery? Thou that abhorrest
idols, dost thou commit sacrilege? Thou that makest thy
boast of the law, through breaking the law dishonourest
thou God?* (Rom. 2:17-23 KJV).

What kind of leader are you?

LED BY DEAD MEN

Along with awakenings and revivals also come great chal-
lenges and stirrings. Even in the middle of the era known as "The
Great Awakening," many leaders refused to grab hold of what
was taking place all around them. Whether they were blind to the
happenings or blatantly rejected a fresh outpouring, they were a
hindrance to many. In either case, they were spiritually dead, and
where there is no life in the leader, there will be no life in the followers. If there is no life in the worship, people will not feel the
presence of God. Without life, there is death. In every meeting, I
tell my team, "When the leader is the last one crying at the altar,
then we will have a revival in America."

Once while George Whitefield was retuning to England
after being in America, he said, "I am greatly persuaded that the
generality of the preachers talk of an unknown, unfelt Christ.
And the reason why congregations have been so dead is because
dead men preach to them."[6]

Have leaders come to the place where what they do is
merely out of habit and necessity than out of joy and with
great rewards? Do they speak of what they do not know? Is it
commonplace for them to fulfill their requirements as leaders
just to get through a Sunday sermon and be done with it until
the following week? How many church leaders are leading
with absolutely no passion in what they believe? The passion-
less are the visionless, and where there is no vision, the people
die (see Prov. 29:18).

Chapter Seven

THE VINEYARD

Now will I sing to my wellbeloved a song of my beloved touching His vineyard. My wellbeloved hath a vineyard in a very fruitful hill: and He fenced it, and gathered out the stones thereof, and planted it with the choicest vine, and built a tower in the midst of it, and also made a winepress therein: and He looked that it should bring forth grapes, and it brought forth wild grapes (Isa. 5:1-2 KJV).

The Word of the Lord came to Isaiah about a vineyard—the Lord's vineyard. Set upon a very fruitful hill, its first-class beauty surpassed all other vineyards. Its hedges were immaculately manicured and a tower and winepress were built in the midst of it.

The description of this vineyard in all its perfection makes me think of Disney World. At Disney World, not one blade of grass seems to be out of place. Not one flower is wilted, and all hedges are neatly trimmed. If you have never been to Disney World, just imagine with me a vineyard of absolute flawlessness and perfection.

Now picture the master of the vineyard coming to stroll among its vines. Impressed with its beauty, he focuses even a little closer on the grapes themselves. He plucks the fruit from the vine, anticipating the savor, but...his expectation quickly turns to disappointment. In an instant, the beauty has lost its appeal. The taste is of sour bitterness. He spits the grape out of his mouth in disgust.

THE CHURCH—A BEAUTIFUL
BUT PURPOSELESS VINEYARD

In 1999, this vineyard message was given to me by the Lord, depicting the American church. The Lord impressed upon me to urgently take this message across the land, in order to prepare the church for what is about to come. The present-day church as a whole needs to reflect the church of Acts. The Book of Acts clearly indicates that Christians didn't preach inside the building, but prayed inside the building and preached outside the building. Today, we practice exactly the opposite. The majority of people being preached to are those who already know Jesus, and those we pray for are people who don't know Jesus. However, we should be praying with people who do know Jesus and preaching to people who don't know Jesus. Now consider what the church should and should not be doing in regard to the seemingly beautiful vineyard.

I want you to envision a church that has everything it could possibly need. Its beauty is noticed by everyone passing and is the talk of the town. Light reflects off the breathtaking steeple, and its pillars stand mighty in strength. It's gorgeous. On Sunday the parking lot is full as people pour into the house of God. As you walk into the foyer and make your way to the sanctuary, you stand in awe as the size of the room seems to overtake you. Moving forward, you take note of the cushioned seats that welcome you and other people finding their way down the aisles. The picture is perfect.

And this is the picture of the American church today. We have air condition and heat. We have earmuffs and sound booths. We have spotlights and microphones. We have the latest technology and all the creature comforts. We have it all. Everything is nice and proper. And is there anything wrong with that? No. God is a God of blessing and more than enough. He didn't mind that the Laodicean church was blessed. God wants to bless us as well. But the purpose of the vineyard, the church, is to produce grapes. That is the actual reason for the vineyard. It is not just supposed to look good; it must have a purpose.

When the master of the house came down to taste of the purpose, he was greatly disappointed and frustrated. Although the outside beauty of the vineyard or the church was exquisite, and it was located on a fruitful hill, it still did not produce choice, delicious-tasting grapes.

UNFRUITFUL IN A FREE AND FERTILE LAND

Shouldn't we as a church be producing the best grapes? Shouldn't we be producing the best Holy Ghost Christians who are radically and passionately on fire for Jesus Christ? We live on a very fruitful hill—our country has been blessed with freedoms of speech and religion. We have the opportunity to go knock on doors and tell people about Jesus. We need not fear that we will suffer physical persecution for our faith. And yet we produce little or no fruit.

A flyer once caught my attention in a church that read, "Please pray for the persecuted church." I agree that praying is important and essential for the Christian life, but perhaps we should first think about the reason for which this church is being persecuted. Are they suffering persecution because they are being affective? Could they be experiencing attacks because their message is reaching thousands and piercing hearts in a forbidden land? I asked the pastor about the purpose of the flyer, and he replied, "We need to pray for the persecuted church." I said, "Pastor, I'm not praying for the persecuted church. I am praying for the unpersecuted church." Pray for the persecuted church? Why? The Bible says that all those who live godly in Christ will suffer much persecution. They must be doing something right. In fact, they are praying for the unpersecuted church. I've heard of a foreign pastor coming to America and after observing the church scene, he commented, "It's amazing what the church can build without God." Pray for the unpersecuted church.

The people who come for a taste at a church producing wild grapes will not be delighted to find a welcoming sweetness, but will reject and turn from an unappealing sourness. When the lost come into your church looking for an answer, are they tasting and indulging, or are they tasting and spitting? A heartrending fact about most people in America is that they have already been to a church before. They have stepped inside the four walls and leave still lost and searching, rejecting what they see, hear, and feel. Isn't it sad that people can come looking for an answer in the house of God and not receive one? Outsiders walk into a church to receive but leave empty-handed. The lost remain lost.

On the contrary, the church needs to be a place of answers. The church needs to be a place where one can come home. It should be more than just a service. People who walk in should feel the presence of the Almighty God. There should be a stirring in their hearts by what is taking place. When the lost walk into the church, they should see, hear, and feel something that intrigues them and something that pulls on their very inner soul. The world is supposed to look at the church body and say, "I want that!"

A VINEYARD DESTROYED

*And now, O inhabitants of Jerusalem, and men of Judah, judge, I pray you, betwixt Me and My vineyard. What could have been done more to My vineyard, that I have not done in it? Wherefore, when I looked that it should bring forth grapes, brought it forth wild grapes? And now go to; I will tell you what I will do to My vineyard: I will take away the hedge thereof, and it shall be eaten up; and break down the wall thereof, and it shall be trodden down: and I will lay it waste: it shall not be pruned, nor digged; but there shall come up briers and thorns: I will also command the clouds that they rain no rain upon it. For the vineyard of the Lord of hosts is the house of Israel, and the men of Judah his pleasant plant: **and He looked for judgment, but behold oppression; for righteousness, but behold a cry** (Isa. 5:3-7 KJV, emphasis added).*

"He looked for judgment, but behold oppression." He looked for judgment in His church, but found oppression. Do you realize that the church is supposed to have conviction, yet without oppressing people? It is supposed to be a place where people change and where their needs are met. This should be the vision of the church as a whole in America. I believe the formality and structure of the American church will change in the next few years. God will awaken us and set us on a new course. Instead of being a church that is focused on the internal, we will be focused on the external. Church should be more than just services and extracurricular activities such as bake sales, car washes, leadership and seminar trainings. We cannot continue to eat the fruit of the land without producing a harvest. It is time to get back to the primary purpose of God's people, and that is winning souls for the Kingdom.

GOD'S NEW VINEYARD

God wants a producing church! He wants a vineyard that is plentiful and abundant and whose taste is sweet. Our job as Christians is to show Jesus as He really is and to introduce people to our Savior. People should taste and see that He is good, like honey on their lips. In this Scripture of Isaiah, God came to the vineyard to hack away the mess and put things in their proper order. Church, there is nothing wrong with having manicured hedges, exquisite furnishings, and up-to-date technology; but the purpose of the vineyard is to produce proper grapes. If it doesn't produce proper grapes, do we really need the vineyard? And if we don't need the vineyard, then the vineyard is just taking up space.

Most churches in America are just taking up space and actually hurting the cause of Christ. People are wise to the religiosity. It disgusts and disappoints them. They have tried church, and it has done nothing for them...because they did not meet Jesus. When they do meet Him, they will want what we have.

Chapter Eight

A DAILY HOUSE
OF PRAYER

I believe that in these last days the church will look quite different. The churches that have been touched by this fresh move of God are already changing the way they conduct their services. They are no longer following the status quo of the American church but are finding that once they are yielded to the moving of the Holy Spirit, there is a new freedom that replaces the once formatted service.

Throughout the 28 chapters of Acts, God gives a general guideline as to what the early church looked like and did. They were a church that moved. They knew what it meant to worship. They were a church that changed the world. They were not a ritualistic church that acted more like a social club than a house of God. Unfortunately, the format recorded in the Book of Acts church cannot be found in most church services taking place in the United States today. There are churches now where a person would have a hard time differentiating them from an Elks Club. You can go to church and look at a bulletin and find that there are often more social activities and outings than times set aside to pray and seek the Father's face or spent in pure worship of God the Father.

The cry of the Lord's heart was that His house was known to all nations as a house of prayer. Sadly, we have made it something so different. Even within the Charismatic movement the church has become a house of preaching. But the Lord never said it should be a house of preaching, but a house of prayer. As mentioned previously, the modern-day church preaches inside and prays outside. Conversely, the Book of Acts church prayed inside and preached outside. The main purpose of the upper room was to convene with God, cry out for mercy and grace for all people, ask for power, and then have the Holy Spirit in manifestation touch and fill up his church. No wonder we have a destitute land. We have had a destitute church, devoid of the Holy Spirit.

A SICK CHURCH IN A DYING WORLD

In the Book of Acts, we read about a church that was extremely public, definitely not what you would call seeker sensitive. This church and its followers were very committed and overwhelmingly bold in their faith, to the extent that many were thrown in prison and martyred. Where is that kind of Christian today?

The church has obviously become a quiet voice in our land. Where Christians once held most major positions and most of our government and military leaders were public with their faith, now we find their voice is almost non-existent and the Body of Christ motionless. Why is the church sleeping?

Just as too much sleep is not healthy for the body, so a constant state of sleep is unhealthy for the church. The Lord revealed to me that the reason the church sleeps is because it is sick. When someone is physicaly sick, the thing he needs most in order to get better is sleep. Thus, the church sleeps because it is sick. What causes sickness? Medical science will tell you that almost 90 percent of health problems are caused by malnutrition or improper eating habits. As the saying goes, "You are what you eat." The reason the church is sick is because we have been eating the wrong stuff. We've been indulging in all the candy and junk food we can get our hands on.

ME, ME, ME

As a youth, I grew up learning all about *my* healing, *my* provision, *my* joy, and *my* peace. It was all about me, myself, and

I. I constantly heard about the perks of being a Christian; very seldom did I hear about the works. *You mean, I had to do something?* Fortunately, I realized that Christianity is not about me. Our lives are supposed to be hidden in Christ, and we are supposed to be dead to the things of self.

One of the reasons Jesus our Lord walked this life was to give us an example. He seldom talked about Himself, nor was He caught up in His own world. He always did those things that pleased His Father. Even as a young boy, Jesus was found doing the work of His Father.

As a church, we have been eating junk food far too long; we've been entirely focused on ourselves and blinded to God and others. Does God want to give me healing, provision, joy, peace, and other blessings? Yes, undeniably yes. However, He wants our attention entirely toward Him, and our hearts devoted to the cause of Christ on this earth. Then all those things that we need will be added unto us.

How dare we as church leaders stand before people and shallowly go on and on about what God wants to do for them and how the church can serve them! We have made everything about us. How ashamed we should be. We will never live a fulfilling life until we discover that it's not about what God can do for you or me; it's about what we can do for God.

Sadly, we have trained a group of people to come for the regularly scheduled services every Sunday, to be served. And yet, they seldom offer their services, inside or outside the church, during the week. Many people will spend hours and hours satisfying their own desires with all kinds of entertainment, and then come to church and outstretch their hands to heaven to receive even more. And the church continues to feed this selfish attitude of always receiving, instead of giving. Oh, we might occasionally preach a message about giving—"give so you will get blessed." People may give, but with a selfish heart of receiving for themselves and not as an offering unto the Lord of hosts. We have taught wrong motivations through the "prosperity message," and consequently, many have gone into debt.

The key is getting our eyes off our own circumstances and giving to Him because of who He is and because He is worthy. He is our greatest example—God so loved the world that He gave. I believe we should repent for teaching these things that build churches, but not the Kingdom. That's why we have a sleeping church devoid of any works; that's why the world sees us the way they do. We are what we eat, and we need to change our diet.

THE FEAR OF THE LORD

The fear of the Lord is the beginning of wisdom (Prov. 9:10, emphasis added)

*...what does the Lord your God ask of you but to **fear** the Lord your God, to walk in all His ways, to love Him, to serve the Lord your God with all your heart and with all your soul, and to observe the Lord's commands and decrees that I am giving you today for your own good* (Deut. 10:12-13, emphasis added).

As Christians our job is to love the sinners and hate the sin. It is to share the message of the gospel and bring God's hope to the world. Once people grasp what salvation is about and have an understanding of the greatness of the love of God for them, many will desire salvation.

However, the obstacle we now face is not only that people are not sharing their faith, but they continue to live their lives by the standards of the world. There is no difference from the way they live than that of the unsaved. As "Christians" we have a tendency to have more passion about golf, football, shopping, and entertainment, while at the same time, we point at the world saying, "Get saved!" All the while they look at us and say, "What makes you different about you from me?"

As God has His arms open wide drawing the lost to Himself, people in the church have the responsibility to set a higher standard—that of standing in awe and reverence of God. The fear of God must come into the church house and we must grasp what He did for us. How dare we honor Him with our lips while our hearts are far from Him! We have taken the things of God too lightly. We have lost our fear of God.

Let me explain what it means to "fear" the Lord. When I say "fear," I don't mean that we have to worry that God is going to come down and beat us over the head when we misbehave. The fear of the Lord relates to the word "reverence." Whatever God says to do, we must do, for He is a holy God and knows that it is in our best interest to live righteously. For instance, Jesus said, "Preach the gospel to the world." But do you know how many people I have heard say, "I'm not called to do that"? That statement literally stuns me. What do you mean you're not called to do that? Don't you have a fear of God? You should have a holy fear of God that when He says, "Go into all the world," you get up and go.

As Jesus hung on the cross, the thief to the left called out, "If Thou be Christ save Thyself and us!" His focus was totally on himself. The other thief on the cross responded, "Dost thou not fear God, seeing thou art in the same condemnation? And we indeed justly; for we receive the due reward of our deeds: but this man hath done nothing amiss." It should be a fearful thing to go before the Lord seeking selfish desires. Likewise, it should be a fearful thing to receive the due reward of our deeds.

The fear of the Lord must come on the church. For far too long we have been living the Doris Day doctrine—*Que sera, sera* —"Whatever will be, will be." I've never read those words in the Word of God. Contrarily, Acts 2:41-43 says, "Then they that gladly received his word were baptized…and fear came upon every soul: and many wonders and signs were done by the apostles." People get excited about seeing the Book of Acts signs, wonders, and miracles. They are ready to see blind eyes open and the crippled walk. They want to see cities shaken for the Lord. But are you ready to see people drop dead in church? Consider Ananias and Sapphira. Acts 5:5 says, "And Ananias hearing these words fell down, and gave up the ghost: and great fear came on all them that heard these things" (KJV). Are you amazed at the fear that fell in that place? It was serious. Ananias was carried out because he had lied. Three hours later, his wife, Sapphira, also fell dead at Peter's feet. "And great fear came upon all the church, and upon as many as heard these things (Acts 5:11 KJV).

I prophesy that these signs and wonders will come again. Eyes and ears will pop open—not in Africa, not in Nigeria, but in America! This same Book of Acts church is coming again. An awareness of God is coming when we actually believe that where two or three are gathered in His name, He is there in the midst of them. Just as in the days of Wesley, Whitefield, Edwards, and Finney, a fear of God or a trembling anointing is coming to the United States of America.

WE NEED TO MEET DAILY

The last-day church will be a church that is constantly filled with the Holy Spirit. Our ministry's vision is not one where we meet two or three times a week, have a few services to get people fired up, and then leave. No. Our meetings take place every day. The Book of Acts church met daily. Daily seems abnormal to most people, but it was business as usual in those days. Special conferences weren't held here and there. They were a radical unified people that met together every day. I believe that this one point of meeting every day could be the single most important revelation in the Book of Acts. It specifically says in Acts 2:46 that they met daily, and consequently, "the Lord added to the church daily" (Acts 2:47).

Where did we as a church get the idea that we are supposed to meet only on Sundays? As the Body of Christ and believers, we are supposed to be set together for a purpose. If you were to compare a body of believers to a modern-day army, you would probably see more dedication in the army than you would the believers. An army must meet every day in order to become uniformly trained in their tactics and prepared for their tasks. Their training is an everyday occurrence. How much more important is it that we as a church are preparing ourselves as the army of the Lord!

The purpose of meeting every day is to come together and spend time worshiping Him. It is a time where you single-mindedly and completely focus on Him. It is not a time for us, but for Him. We have enough other things taking place in life that focus on ourselves. During these meetings we set our eyes on Him only and not on what He can do for us. We worship Him just because of who He is. As we take the time to worship Him, we celebrate all the ways that the Lord has worked in and through individual lives that very day.

Testimony Time

Often praises and offerings of thanksgiving are too numerous to count, and there are many testimonies of lives that have been changed, healed, and restored.

As people are sharing their testimonies from the outreaches that are held each day, they bring completed cards with names of those they shared Jesus with that day and who accepted Him into their hearts. People throughout the congregation leave their seats and make way to the front, full of excitement about the lives that have been changed. There are even some who can barely contain themselves and practically bolt out of their seats to the front, ready to share. Once all the cards are gathered, every single name is read off as we rejoice over those who encountered Christ that day and week. There have been times where we have had 10 cards and other times when we've had over a thousand. Then, when all the cards have been read, we throw them into the air and watch as they disperse covering the floor of the sanctuary. By the end of the revival, the floor is flooded with thousands of cards. It is an amazing and spectacular sight to see as each card represents a life that has been touched. It is a visual reminder of why we are here on this earth—to seek and save the lost.

The most amazing thing of all is that God knows each soul who was touched that day, and heaven rejoices when just one lost soul has come home. As people testify during the service they share what the Lord has done *through* them. Whereas most testimonies in modern churches are about what the Lord has done *to* them or *for* them, we must focus on what He will do *through* us.

We tell people every night that church is not all about you! Church is about HIM. We are not supposed to come to get—a message widely spread to those inside the church. Instead, church needs to be more like the practice field. Whatever we do inside is our practice time for what we must do outside. We need to redirect our focus from getting inside to going outside into this thing we call "life." We must teach people that it is truly all about giving, just as Jesus came to give, and not get. When it is all about giving inside, it will be all about giving outside.

THE LATTER HOUSE WILL BE GREATER THAN THE FORMER

Every night presents something different. There are times when we preach and other nights where people are exhorted. God moves differently every night, and you never know the direction He will move. That is why it is so important to yield to Him. Every day we must allow the Holy Spirit to fill up His people again and again. We realize the importance of being full of God and spend time crying out to Him, just as Luke 11 describes we are to do.

As you go out into the world each day, we need to daily refill ourselves with more of Him. Unfortunately, most Christians who are praying for more haven't done anything with the more they received the last time they prayed. For a pitcher of water to be refilled, it must first be emptied out. Our God is not a wasteful God. As vessels, we need to continually pour out what we have already been given. And so, many revivals come to an end, because we don't know what to do with what we have been given or what we should be crying out for.

The last-day army of God is beginning to look much different. The patterns and the ways of doing church are changing. Messages from the pulpit are changing. The idea of the comfortable, board-pleasing messages are coming to an end. There will be no more cookie bake sales and car washes. The latter house will be greater than the former. People will learn what it means to sacrifice. Just as fire came down in the Old Testament to burn up the sacrifice, so will it come down on the sacrifice again. God loves the smell of burning flesh. It is when we surrender ourselves completely to Him that we allow Him to move in our lives even more. In this last day, there will be radical, unselfish givers with no impure motives of giving in order to receive. Their eyes will be completely off themselves, and their lives will be totally dedicated to the Father's business. They will be relentless in their pursuit of their lost coin, the lost sheep, and the prodigal sons and daughters.

Chapter Nine

VISIONS

God desires to be in constant communion with His children, and one of His methods of communication is through visions. The Old and New Testaments are filled with episode after episode of God-given visions to grab the attention of many.

THE BREATH OF HEAVEN

Having breath means having life, and with it the ability to move. When hundreds of thousands begin moving, an army of God will come forth; and with that army, a new vision will fall into place. To fully understand the message of this call, you need to read Ezekiel chapter 37, where God reveals a vision to the prophet Ezekiel.

> *The hand of the Lord was upon me, and carried me out in the spirit of the Lord, and set me down in the midst of the valley which was full of bones, and caused me to pass by them round about: and, behold, there were very many in the open valley; and lo, they were very dry. And He said unto me, Son of man, can these bones live? And I answered, O Lord God, Thou knowest. Again He said unto me, **Prophesy upon these bones,** and say unto them, O ye dry bones, **hear the word of the Lord.** Thus saith the Lord God unto these bones; Behold, I will cause breath to enter into you, and ye shall live: and I will lay sinews upon you, and will bring up flesh upon you, and cover you with skin, and put breath in*

you, and ye shall live; and ye shall know that I am the Lord. So I prophesied as I was commanded: and as I prophesied, there was a noise, and behold a shaking, and the bones came together, bone to his bone. And when I beheld, lo, the sinews and the flesh came up upon them, and the skin covered them above: but there was no breath in them. Then said He unto me, Prophesy unto the wind, prophesy, son of man, and say to the wind, Thus saith the Lord God; Come from the four winds, O breath, and breathe upon these slain, that they may live. So I prophesied as He commanded me, and the breath came into them, and they lived, and stood up upon their feet, an exceeding great army. Then He said unto me, Son of man, these bones are the whole house of Israel: behold, they say, Our bones are dried, and our hope is lost: we are cut off for our parts. Therefore prophesy and say unto them, Thus saith the Lord God; Behold, O My people, I will open your graves, and cause you to come up out of your graves, and bring you into the land of Israel. And ye shall know that I am the Lord, when I have opened your graves, O My people, and brought you up out of your graves, and shall put My spirit in you, **and ye shall live,** *and I shall place you in your own land: then shall ye know that I the Lord have spoken it, and performed it, saith the Lord* (Ezek. 37:1-14 KJV, emphasis added).

To gain a full understanding of this message, we must first know a little about the prophet Ezekiel and the time in which he lived. The name *Ezekiel* means "God strengthened."[7] And this is exactly what God did. God strengthened him for the task assigned to him. Ezekiel, called to be a prophet of the Lord at the age of 30, spent years proclaiming God's message to the Jews. The period was around 593 B.C. At this time, Ezekiel warned the Jews in Jerusalem about the outcome of turning their backs on God. Following Ezekiel's admonition, destruction came, and Jerusalem fell. During this time though, Ezekiel's message changed from destruction to expectation, as those who were exiled from Jerusalem returned, and life as they knew it, was restored. It is in chapter 37 where God began to show Ezekiel the process of restoration.

"THEM BONES ARE GONNA RISE AGAIN"

In the very beginning of this chapter, Ezekiel was brought to a valley and led back and forth to view that valley. This was not just something he would casually glimpse at and forget. No, this was something that would forever amaze him. Pacing through this valley, he saw before him a great amount of bones—not just any bones, but human bones—dry bones that had been lying there for quite some time. Unexpectedly, the Lord asked Ezekiel, "Can these bones live?" Had anyone else been asked that question, the most likely response would have been, "There ain't no way!" Yet, Ezekiel knew in his heart that he served the God of the impossible.

Many times when God questions us, our response will reveal our own hearts' condition. Ezekiel responded, "O Sovereign Lord, You alone know." With God all things are possible.

In verse 4, the Lord commanded Ezekiel to prophesy to the bones. Notice that the Lord was very direct and specific with Ezekiel. God instructed him exactly what to do and in detail. The word *prophesy* is an action word. This was something Ezekiel had to do. He had to move and show action. God shifted responsibility to Ezekiel and commanded that He speak to the bones. He never told Ezekiel to talk about the bones. He knew the bones were dead. It was obvious. He asked him to speak life to the bones. In complete obedience, Ezekiel acted and the bones responded.

Immediately, there was a noise, a rattling. The bones that were on the floor of the valley began coming together and taking shape. The amazing thing is that this act, which seems unlikely to us, was simple for God. The human body itself consists of 206 bones. It was like God was putting a puzzle together! Not only did the bone structure itself come together, but God also added all the tendons, muscles, and layers of skin that a human body is made up of. So there before Ezekiel stood a great number of bodies.

Although these bodies were standing, they contained no breath, and without breath life cannot exist. In Genesis 2:7, we see how essential breath is:

> *The Lord God formed the man from the dust of the ground and breathed into his nostrils the breath of life, and the man became **a living being*** (emphasis added).

Following this, the Lord again commanded Ezekiel to speak to the winds, and speak breath into the slain that they may live. In obedience, Ezekiel once again acted, and before him stood an army. Not just any army, but an army full of life!

God used this vision of Ezekiel's to show His plans for the nation of Israel. May we as followers of Christ take this vision of Ezekiel's and apply it to our own lives, for this day and age.

OTHER VISIONS FROM THE SCRIPTURE

Daniel 1:17 says, "To these four young men God gave knowledge and understanding of all kinds of literature and learning. And Daniel could understand *visions* and dreams of all kinds" (emphasis added). Daniel was highly esteemed for being able to interpret dreams and visions. Not only did he interpret dreams and visions, but he himself also had them. Daniel 8:1 says, "In the third year of King Belshazzar's reign, I Daniel, had *a vision*, after the one that already appeared to me" (emphasis added).

In the previous Book, the prophet Ezekiel says, "In the thirtieth year, in the fourth month on the fifth day, while I was among the exiles by the Kebar River, the heavens were opened and I saw *visions* of God" (Ezek. 1:1, emphasis added). Hosea 12:10 states, "I spoke to the prophets, gave them many *visions* and told parables through them" (emphasis added).

The most well-known verse regarding visions is Joel 2:28:

*And afterward, I will pour out My Spirit on all people. Your sons and daughters will prophesy, your old men will dream dreams, your young men will see **visions**. Even on my servants, both men and women, I will pour out My Spirit in those days* (emphasis added).

Through this promise we jump into the New Testament and view Saul while on a journey, experiencing an encounter with Jesus, an encounter that would cost him his sight. Yet God marvelously works and appears to Ananias in a vision. He states in Acts 9:11-12,

*Go to the house of Judas on Straight Street and ask for a man from Tarsus named Saul, for he is praying. In a **vision** he has seen a man named Ananias come and place his hands on him to restore his sight* (emphasis added).

Then in chapter 10, a centurion in the Italian Regiment named Cornelius has a vision at about three in the afternoon. An angel speaks to him and tells him to send men to Joppa to bring back Simon called Peter. At about this same time, Peter, while on a roof praying, sees Heaven open up and a large sheet being let down to earth by its four corners. It is filled with four-footed animals and reptiles and birds. Verse 13-15 says,

Then a voice told him, "Get up, Peter. Kill and eat." "Surely not, Lord!" Peter replied. "I have never eaten anything impure or unclean." The voice spoke to him a second time, "Do not call anything impure that God has made clean."

It is when Peter meets with Cornelius that he understands the meaning of the vision.

*You are well aware that it is against our law for a Jew to associate with a Gentile or visit him. But God has **shown me** that I should not call any man impure or unclean* (Acts 10:28, emphasis added).

Peter has a divine revelation of God's acceptance of all, and because of this revelation, sees that God wants to radically shake the Gentiles.

> *While Peter was still speaking these words, the Holy Spirit*
> *came on all who heard the message. The circumcised believ-*
> *ers who had come with Peter were astonished that the gift of*
> *the Holy Spirit had been poured out even on the Gentiles.*
> *For they heard them speaking in tongues and praising God*
> (Acts 10:44).

Salvation is for everyone who believes—not just for the Jew, not just for the Gentile—but for everyone. The question is, do you believe? Believers are supposed to believe. Joel 3:14 cries out, "Multitudes, multitudes in the valley of decision! For the day of the Lord is near in the valley of decision." This is not a game. This is reality. Jesus came to this earth to seek and save the lost. This is what burned such a fiery passion in the lives of the greatest reformers and revivalists in history. It is what made them weep and cry for nations and what made them shout from the top of their lungs for God's great mercy. It is what made them cry out into the early morning hours and what made them refuse to stop as long as an ear was absent of the gospel truth. It is what desperately burns in my heart as I watch people daily pass by in life's normal routine. My heart is consumed with the thought of many of you who are in the valley of decision. Rise up. Your soul is being fought for. Awaken yourselves. Climb out of that valley into the mountaintops of God.

THE VISION OF THE
AWAKENING OF AMERICA

Evan Roberts had a vision he could not shake and one that sustained him. He saw vast multitudes of people rushing toward the never-ending torment of hell, but felt that God was granting a season to which a hundred thousand would be saved. And because of this vision, he persevered and believed that through his obedience he would see that hundred thousand saved.

This last year God also gave me a vision that stirs so strongly in my soul and will be forever imprinted in my mind. I saw multitudes and multitudes of people. Millions—just like Ezekiel saw. I saw people lying down, face up, with their eyes closed. In my finite way of thinking, I thought they were dead. We have a saying at our ministry that the Book of Acts church *raised* the dead, while the modern-day church is dead. I thought, *God, they're dead, they're dead!* Then from directly behind me I heard a voice. "They're not dead, Tommie. They're not dead. They're only sleeping. We must go wake them up."

I then looked and saw another group of people. It wasn't millions, nor was it thousands. It was a handful. It was a handful of people being raised up. They were passionately crying out night and day. They were crying out for the souls of those sleeping. This army's intense cry was so fervent that it seemed to settle over the multitudes. The noise, like sound waves, hovered above like a blanket. It was similar to the sound of the alarm in the morning in that every time we hear it, it opens our eyes. Now I know what the Lord meant when He said, "Sound the alarm in Zion."

Those crying out were so oblivious to the things of the world and so intent on reaching and awakening the multitudes. The cry continued until an awakening began. The closed eyes slowly began to open.

In this vision, I was underneath them looking up at them, looking up into Heaven. Then I became overwhelmed, for I saw Jesus. He was seated on the throne, yet He wasn't seated as one would sit comfortably. He was seated at the edge of His throne. I actually saw Jesus in that room. (No, I hadn't eaten too much pizza.) He spoke with intensity. He said, "Who will go for Me? Whom shall I send?" The multitudes lying on the ground understood the urgency of the hour when they saw Him seated on His throne. They understood that the time was short.

The apostle Paul says in Romans 13:11, "And that, knowing the time, that now it is high time to awake out of sleep: for now is our salvation nearer than when we believed" (KJV). We must know the time we live in. When your alarm rings, you know it is time to go to work. You understand the reason for the alarm in accordance to the time. When those in this vision understood the time, they said, "Here am I, Lord. Send me." Then they rose up on their feet. Millions and millions of soldiers began to walk into the cities of America. I promised the Lord that I would share this vision in every single church I step into, and that I would tell them that the hour is urgent.

THE VISION OF THE AMERICAN REVOLUTION

The Bible says that in the last days, young men will see visions. Prior to my vision of the awakening of America that I had while in Wisconsin, the Lord granted me another vision while ministering in Michigan. We were in the middle of a revival service, and it was early in the morning around 1:30 AM. There were people prostrate on the ground seeking the face of God, and suddenly it seemed as if I had stepped over into another realm.

Immediately I saw average, ordinary people walking out of their homes. They were people like you would see every day, wearing comfortable, regular clothes. They were coming from everywhere and seemed to be gathering in one place—in what appeared to be a courtyard. Once they all were in the courtyard, there was a sudden sound that echoed throughout the sky and some sort of rumbling. Immediately, everyone who stood in the courtyard formed a line like an army and started marching forward. As they marched ahead, a power of light shone brightly behind them. It produced some kind of energy power like a giant fireball. I asked, "Lord, what is this?" He said, "Tommie, that's how you take America."

That night I pondered the vision, and the Lord gave me understanding. The vision revealed how America was birthed the first time and gained her freedom. When you study the period of 1775-1783 you find ordinary Americans who were desperate for freedom and fought their way to victory in the American Revolution or Revolutionary War. Great Britain had desired to seize control of the 13 colonies and disbanded their rights as individuals. The colonists, longing to separate themselves from the clutches of the king of England, knew that remaining passive would not accomplish their goal. As the king placed taxes on the colonies and did what he could to control the colonists, he found multitudes opposed to his wishes. There were too many who had moved to America for its freedom and benefits.

The king sent troops to gain control of the colonies, yet the colonists resisted. Many took a stand, even though it cost them their lives. From the Battle at Lexington and Concord, to the Battle of Bunker Hill, to Saratoga and Valley Forge, they fought. From Paul Revere warning, "The British are coming, the British are coming," to Patrick Henry yelling, "Give me liberty or give me death," they stood firm. May those same words cry out today, and may we actually mean them.

On July 4, 1776 men such as Benjamin Franklin, John Adams, Thomas Jefferson, John Hancock, and many others signed the Declaration of Independence, declaring as individuals their rights and freedoms no matter what the outcome would be. Many were willing to lay down their lives for this cause of freedom. Isn't that what we all are longing for? In Christ there is freedom, Church! Again I could hear His voice, "Tommie, that's how you take America." It takes people standing up for what they truly believe in. It takes a group of ordinary people, crying out in an extraordinary way, for an extraordinary God to send His power down.

It was sometime later that God gave me another piece of this vision, which happened to be the beginning of it. He showed me a mother and a father, grandma and grandpa, and children on their faces lying prostrate in their house. They were crying out with determination to their God. Suddenly, they got up together and walked out of their home. They walked to the courtyard. They were the normal, ordinary people in the courtyard who had decided that they would not be satisfied with the status of our nation any longer. They were going to gather together and fight for what they believed in.

This would not be a natural kind of fighting, but one done in the Spirit...for our battle is not flesh and blood but against principalities and everything that exalts itself against the knowledge of Christ. It is time to take those things captive! These are individuals who are tired of unwed teen pregnancies, all kinds of sexual perversions over the Internet, and a 60 percent divorce rate in our society. They want their schools back so that their children can learn about the God our nation was founded upon. They want prayer returned to the schools and desire that their kids learn from God-fearing people all around them, both men and women alike. But they understand that men's hearts have to change first before their laws will.

And thus they cry out day and night, night and day, just like the prophet Jeremiah, and weep for mankind. Thus they go into the world, endued with the spirit of Heaven and take their stand for righteousness. They cry out, go out, and give out.

During the Wales 1904 revival, they did just that. They were desperate. They wouldn't take no for an answer, and consequently, they shook their nation. Within weeks God responded. He always responds to the cries of the righteous. "That's how you take America." Those are the people God is awakening in our land in this hour. That's how America was birthed the first time and that's how she will become spiritually born again.

Chapter Ten

THE GREAT AWAKENINGS
AND REFORMATIONS

There once was a cry that resounded across the land from the deepest part of passionate and radical earth shakers. It was a cry that penetrated every heart that heard its message. It was from people who devoted their lives and every waking moment to bringing the message of salvation to a world that was walking blindly off course to a road of destruction. We see it in studying the lives of Martin Luther, Jonathan Edwards, and John Wesley. It was a message that shot through the veins of Charles Finney, Evan Roberts, and George Whitefield. People could not come into the presence of these men of God without coming face-to-face with their own carnality. Flesh would not have dominion, as the Spirit of God divided soul and spirit. Lives were shaken.

This did not come without a price. Each of these great men of the faith had tenacity. They endured much persecution and mockery, but did not fall short of their calling. Through extensive and intense prayer, each of these saints held onto their view of eternity. Whether these men shook a nation or an individual life, their uninhibited message of the gospel ushered in great revivals to this and other nations. A fire was set aflame. All that was needed were vessels, and through these vessels, God poured out. Many were drenched with the dew of heaven, while others remain parched because of their lack of desire.

What was it that enabled these men to see the supernatural? They experienced God's omnipotence as the sick were healed, the lost were found, and sinners were set free. They had an unabashed passion to see their nations repent and turn their hearts to God. They recklessly pursued the heart of God and, as a result, saw a great awakening.

Today, the cry that resounded so many years ago has settled to a quiet hush. But the voices that echoed so loudly must reverberate again. Those sleeping must awaken to the current condition of their own souls. There must be an awakening.

Let's take a look at the lives of these great vessels and see what so drastically set them apart and what birthed within them a cry for the souls of the lost, that the lost might taste of the riches of the heavenly Father.

MEN OF THE BIBLE

Throughout God's Word, we see men and women who had such an unmatched determination and passion for God that nothing could quench their zeal. We read of Stephen standing before the Sanhedrin, revealing the legacy of God's hand throughout history, proclaiming in Acts 7:51-53:

You stiff-necked people, with uncircumcised hearts and ears. You are just like your fathers. You always resist the Holy Spirit! Was there ever a prophet your fathers did not persecute? They even killed those who predicted the coming of the Righteous One. And now you have betrayed and murdered Him—you who have received the law that was put into effect through angels but have not obeyed it.

Unhindered and with great boldness, Stephen shouted out the oracles of God, regardless of the outcome, and it cost him his life. Unbeknownst to him, God was working on one of his persecutor's hearts, a man named Saul. It was through Stephen's martyrdom that Saul was matched with a passion conflicting his own, yet just as tremendous. Ironically, God gripped Saul's heart to the point where his zeal for persecuting

Christians was transformed into a zeal for becoming a Christian, even to the point of abandoning his Jewish upbringing and religious ways, and being rejected by his own. Saul, later known as Paul, became one of the most influential persons in the New Testament.

Look at Daniel—a man known for prayer; a man who got down on his knees three times a day and prayed facing the city of Jerusalem; a man who faithfully prayed, regardless that a decree had been established arresting any person who would pray to anyone other than the king. Unabashed, he continued praying to his Lord. Lions would not strike enough fear to convince him that his God was not more than enough. The same was true of Shadrach, Meshach, and Abednego, men of superior standing who refused to bow to an image of gold, unwilling to deny their God. On and on throughout the Word we see it. We see it with Jonah, Nehemiah, Noah, Moses, Samson, David, and more. The list goes on and on. Throughout history individuals were driven with an unstoppable fuel. Regardless of those around, the declaration was clear: They would not be set back nor let their fire burn out.

MARTIN LUTHER

In Martin Luther we see this same unstoppable force. The whole nation of Germany was thrown into an uproar—never had there been someone to take a stand like Martin Luther. Luther defied the religious undertakings of the church of the day that insisted that indulgences be sold in accordance to the forgiveness of sins. Indulgences were connected with the pope's ability to allow the forgiveness of sins. Luther was aghast. In no way would he conform to this religious teaching nor allow himself to be melted and molded into this philosophy. No! With boldness, Luther picked up the torch and proclaimed what many were afraid to. Luther spoke, "If a sinner was truly contrite, he received complete forgiveness. The pope's absolution had no value in and for itself."[8] Not only did he speak this in defiance, but he also took the liberty to nail his theses on the church at Wittenberg.

Obviously, this was not seeker-sensitive religion like we have today. Luther was that diamond in the rough, the one who shouted his resolve. Nothing could contain his zeal, not even the threat of his own life. When it came time for him to appear before the "diet," Luther stood. *The Biography of Martin Luther* states: "All Germany was moved by his heroism; his journey resembled a triumph; the threats of enemies and the anxiety of friends alike failed to move him. His appearance and demeanor before the diet, and the firmness with which he held his ground, and refused to retract, all make a striking picture."[9] For three truths did Luther stand: that man is justified by faith alone, believers have direct access to God through the Lord Jesus Christ, and the Bible is the sole source of faith and authority for a Christian.[10]

Do you stand unashamedly for the truths that lie deep within your heart, or do you hide your face when someone mentions the name of Jesus? Do you cringe when someone takes the Lord's name in vain, or are you laughing right along with them? Romans 1:16 states, "I am not ashamed of the gospel, because it is the power of God for the salvation of everyone who believes: first for the Jew, then for the Gentile." May you never be ashamed of the One who gave His all for you!

JONATHAN EDWARDS

Humanity today is still feeling the rippling effect left by possibly the greatest theologian and philosopher America has ever known—Jonathan Edwards.

Jonathan Edwards was nurtured in a home where godliness abounded. His father, Rev. Timothy Edwards, was a congregational minister for 60 years. His grandfather, Rev. Solomon Stoddard, was the minister of the Congregational Church in Northampton, Massachusetts. Having a family solidly grounded in the Word, Jonathan later produced what had become so much a part of him. It is said that at the age of nine, Edwards wrote a paper about the nature of souls, and at twelve was writing about revivals.

Edwards was a man who loved his solitude and his moments of prayer. Many times he would surround himself with the beauty of God's creation where he would get away and reflect, and allow God to infiltrate his heart. As a little boy, he built a prayer booth in a swamp with his classmates so that he could have a place to go to pray. It was when he made himself absent to the processions of society and retreated to quiet places to pray, that he often experienced the awesomeness and majesty of God. Edwards was constantly in awe of God and found it such a privilege to serve God and to be used by Him. While reading the Scriptures, an even deeper awareness of God seemed to drop in his spirit.

Now unto the King eternal, immortal, invisible, the only wise God, be honor and glory forever and ever. Amen (1 Tim. 1:17 KJV).

Even at the heart of revivals, Edwards never lost sight of what they were about, or who would get the glory. During great moves, revivals should always point to Jesus. The Holy Spirit never points to a person, only to God. In one of his journals he wrote,

Once, as I rode out into the woods for my health, in 1737 having alighted from my horse in a retired place, as my manner commonly has been, to walk for divine contemplation and prayer, I had a view, that for me was extraordinary, of the glory of the Son of God as Mediator between God and man, and his wonderful, great, full, pure and sweet grace and love and meek and gentle condescension...which continued as near as I can judge, about an hour: which kept me the greater part of the time in a flood of tears, and weeping aloud....[11]

Are you tasting of the greatness of God such as Edwards did? Do you take time to enjoy who He is and allow the grandeur of Him to sink into the very depths of your soul? Once you do, it will bring you to the place of absolute surrender.

Jonathan not only had the benefits of being brought up in a spiritual home, but also the privilege of being raised in an educated home. This came as no struggle for Edwards. The man was undeniably a child prodigy. In the year of 1716, Edwards enrolled at Yale University just before the age of 13. Upon entering, he had already knew Latin, Greek, and Hebrew. In 1720, at the age of 17, Edwards received his B.A.. It was at this time in his life that he also began to prepare for the ministry, feeling called by God. In 1727, Edwards married Sarah Pierrepont of New Haven. She was a delight to Edwards as she found joy and pleasure being in God's creation and supporting her husband in his endeavors. Their marriage was an example to many and even impressed George Whitefield when visiting during the Great Awakening. Together they had 11 children who became figures who impacted history.

After many more years of preparation and experience, Edwards was ordained as assistant minister to his grandfather's church in Northampton. It was here that Edwards delved into his studies and sermon preparation. Time was essential. With much anticipation and without regard, Edwards spent over 13 hours a day in study and prayer. With a passion and intensity and a dedication to his beliefs, he began to shift the climate of the era of the day.

God birthed many sermons within him that, with God's mighty hand, began to spark a spirit of revival throughout the community. Suddenly people were becoming conscious of their own souls. Through his sermons, many souls were converted. He spoke to them with such a vivid imagination that his hearers were drawn in, almost feeling that they were experiencing much of what he talked about. With his sermons spreading like wildfire, people were hearing the truth from all directions. Some of his best-known sermons are entitled: "The Distinguishing Marks of a Work of the Spirit of God," "Some Thoughts Concerning the Present Revival," "The Religious Affections," and "Sinners in the Hands of an Angry God."

Once, while preaching his sermon, "Sinners in the Hands of an Angry God," people were said to have rolled on the floor and cried out in anguish to the Lord, feeling that they were sliding into the very pit of hell.[12] Before that day ended, over 500 were saved. He was very unyielding to the fact that true Christianity was comprised of a love for God and holiness, and was against fanaticism or any form of false belief.

As Jonathan Edwards continued to see revivals spring up in the New England area, he was intrigued by what he was hearing of the man George Whitefield. Inquiring that he come to visit the town of Northampton in 1740 he wrote,

Rev. Sir,

My request to you is that in your intended journey through New England next summer you would be pleased to visit Northampton. I hope it is not wholly from curiosity that I desire to see and hear you in this place, but I apprehend, from what I have heard, that you are one that has blessing of heaven attending you wherever you go, and I have a great desire, if it be the will of God that such blessings as attends your person and labours may descend on this town. Indeed I am fearful whether you will not be disappointed in New England, and will have less success here than in other places. We who have dwelt in a land that has been distinguished with light, and have long enjoyed the gospel, and have be glutted with it, have despised it, are I fear more hardened than most of those places where you have preached hitherto…. I hope, if God spares my life, to see something of that salvation of God in New England, which He has now begun in a benighted, wicked and miserable world and age and in the most guilty of nations. It has been a refreshment of soul that I have heard of one raised up in the Church of England to revive the mysterious, spiritual, despised and exploded doctrines of the gospel, and full of a spirit of zeal for the promotion of real, vital piety, whose labourers have been attended with such success.[13]

Edwards longed to see revival hit New England. There were various accounts of smaller awakenings previous to this letter he wrote to Whitefield, but soon afterward, what is now known as the Great Awakening, would explode with the founding work being laid by people such as Edwards.

In 1750, Edwards was removed as head of his church because of his definite stand concerning what was called the "Half-Way Covenant." This was a covenant that was institutionalized by his grandfather that stated if the parents were "Christians," then the children could participate in communion as well as baptism. However, in no way did Edwards feel that people should participate unless they were genuine converts themselves. Individuals could not ride on the coattails of their parents. They were to be held accountable for themselves. He would not allow this measure of "works" to fill the church up with unsaved people unwilling to truly dedicate their lives to Christ. He would not settle for shallowness of heart.

GEORGE WHITEFIELD

"O that my head were waters, O that mine eyes were a fountain of tears, that I might weep day and night for the slain of the daughter of my people" (Jer. 9:1 KJV). These words George Whitefield knew well. Whitefield was an English evangelist in the 1700s who through intense preaching and divine providence reached thousands with the gospel message not only in England, but America as well. I am sure that as George Whitefield discovered the Bible at an early age and sat up at night devouring its words, He had no concept as to the extremes that God would use him.

Unlike Evan Roberts, George Whitefield was known for his oratory skills and his ability to draw thousands to hear him preach. It is estimated that tens of thousands could hear him as he preached boldly in a spacious area. Even though he did not have the use of microphones, as in our era, this man's words gushed forth from within his own bosom and grabbed the attention of thousands. How a man could have such a thunder-ing voice was truly a gift from God.

Not only would people tremble at the strength of His voice and the passion with which he spoke, but under the anointing of the Holy Spirit, lives could not remain the same. I imagine that no one could walk away from these meetings without the Holy Spirit burning in their hearts. In Luke 24:32, the disciples real-ized they had been walking with Jesus and said, "Were not our hearts burning within us while He talked with us on the road and opened the Scriptures to us?" When one walks with Jesus and encounters Him, the heart recognizes it. A heart will either burn with passion for God and be aware of His voice, or it will burn with conviction as the Holy Spirit desires to burn away the dross in one's life. Burning is the process of refinement. As gold is refined and burned, the impurities rise to the top and are scraped off. God, a consuming fire, desires to accomplish this process in our lives as well. Whitefield recognized this and so did the thousands who gathered.

God did something incredible through this man, and on more than one continent. From England to America, nations were revived. Nothing brought George Whitefield to a standstill. His voice was known, and he proclaimed all that was birthed in His soul. His burden weighed so heavily for people that it is said he spoke over 18,000 sermons in his lifetime, which averaged around 500 a year or 10 a week. If ever there was a man who spent every moment of his day ministering to someone and pouring out his heart till there was no breath left in his body, George Whitefield was that man. He was totally devoted to his Lord. Whitefield not only preached, but also acted. While in England, He saved money to provide for the poor and needy, especially the orphans in America.

In Whitefield's sermon, "Marks of a True Conversion," he stated:

When I see such a congregation as this, if my heart is in a proper frame, I feel myself ready to lay down my life, to be instrumental only to save one soul. It makes my heart bleed within me, it makes me sometimes most unwilling to preach, lest that word that I hope will do good, may increase the damnation of any, and perhaps of a great part of the auditory, through their own belief. [14]

It is said that Whitefield proclaimed Christ up until a few hours before his death. While traveling through the New England states, I had the opportunity to see where Whitefield preached one of his last sermons. It was at a church in Newburyport, Massachusetts. I could almost envision him standing in the church and the congregation seated before him—a congregation seated, not with deaf ears, but with ears attentive to every word that proceeded out of his mouth. What may have seemed like a small church in this day and age, was most likely running over with people eager to hear the message and be touched by Jesus.

At this very same church is recorded much of the history of George Whitefield. Underneath the pulpit of the church is where he is buried. As I sat next to his coffin, the anointing was tangible. There was still great power in his bones, I believe, like those of Elisha. Second Kings 13:21 says, "Once while some Israelites were burying a man, suddenly they saw a band of raiders; so they threw the man's body into Elisha's tomb. When the body touched Elisha's bones, the man came to life and stood up on his feet." The man stood up!

Being right where Whitefield was buried was unreal. It was a secluded place, and not full of much glamour. There were not thousands flocking to see where his remains lie, but Whitefield's memory and impact continue to resonate. You can still sense the power of God when standing in that place. We pray many more George Whitefield's be awakened in America.

JOHN WESLEY

John Wesley's life was defined by the intimacy of prayer. He knew that for a person to step into the realms of the supernatural and to watch God work the marvelous required a oneness between him and his Lord that could only be bridged through prayer. No person on the face of this earth can radically shake a nation without being engulfed in the throngs of prayer. His preaching was bold and forthright. His mission was not to give sweet sermons and pat everyone on the back. No! He was driven to tear down any form of religiosity to bring about a heart that resided in the simple truth that Christ was the only Way. Wesley was committed to making sure that others understood the Scriptures, from the depths of God's love to the result of rejecting His grace. In his sermon, "On the Holy Spirit," preached in 1736 at St. Mary's in Oxford, Wesley wrote,

> *Well may a man ask his own heart, whether it is able to admit the Spirit of God. For where that divine Guest enters, the laws of another world must be observed: The body must be given up to martyrdom, or spent in the Christian warfare, as unconcernedly as if the soul were already provided of its house from heaven; the goods of this world must be parted with as freely, as if the last fire were to seize them tomorrow; our neighbour must be loved as heartily as if he were washed from all his sins, and demonstrated to be a child of God by the resurrection from the dead. The fruits of the Spirit must not be mere moral virtues, calculated for the comfort and decency of the present life; but holy dispositions, suitable to the instincts of a superior life already begun.* [15]

To want all of God was the life John Wesley so fervently embraced. The Divine Guest was truly a part of his life, and the law of heaven was apparent in his life.

CHARLES FINNEY

An inquisitive heart and a feeling of restlessness is what compelled Charles Finney to search into the mysteries of the gospel and discover the authenticity of the Word. Having never experienced a religious atmosphere in his early years, he was not aware of what it meant to be in constant communion with God. The only privilege of religion he had came from traveling preachers, which possessed no sense of passion that would make anyone long to change from his ways and accept their teachings. It wasn't until Finney's late 20's that the scales covering his eyes slowly began falling away to unveil the truth that he longed to embrace. Finney said, "I do not think I heard half a dozen sermons in English during my stay in New Jersey, which was about three years. Thus when I went to Adams to study law, I was almost as ignorant of religion as a heathen. I had been brought up mostly in the woods. I had very little regard to the Sabbath, and had no definite knowledge of religious truth."[16]

Yet isn't it just like God to take the unlikely things of the world to confound the wise. In the midst of Finney's intense study of law, He came across another Book of Law—the Bible. Expecting to draw from it, as others, for its authority, he found himself submerged into its writings and desired to have an understanding of its scriptures. Thus his search began. It was a search that threw Finney into a turmoil of questions and concerns as he sought answers for three years. At the end of these years, Finney came face-to-face with a decision. As he states: "After struggling in that way for some two or three years, my mind became quite settled that whatever mystification there might be either in my own or in my pastor's mind, or in the mind of the church, the Bible was, nevertheless, the true Word of God. This being settled, I was brought face-to-face with the question whether I would accept Christ as presented in the Gospel, or pursue a worldly course of life. At this period, in my mind, as I have since known, was so much impressed by the Holy Spirit, that I could not long leave this question unsettled; nor could I long hesitate between the two courses of life presented to me."[17]

We all are confronted with this same choice at one time or another. It is not a choice to throw in the wind and leave for tomorrow. Time is not something to cast aside in ignorance. Eternity is at stake. There are two courses—that is the pointed truth. To reject one is to accept the other. To accept one is to reject the other. It is simply to choose between life and death. Yet do not be deceived. What may seem like "life" in this world can tragically end in death in the world to come. A.W. Tozer once said, "A spiritual kingdom lies all about us, enclosing us, embracing us, altogether within reach of our inner selves, waiting for us to recognize it."[18]

As a person reading this book, it is time for you to recognize the condition of your own soul and what God is doing all around you. Do not be foolish and miss the One who came to redeem and save and grant you life. He desires to snatch you from hell and its entanglements. Yet you must choose. You! Choose as Finney did and so many who have experienced God's merciful hand. Before the cry of revival was bursting out of Finney's lungs, he had to be immersed in his own personal revival until God's Word was deeply embedded in his heart and he was prepared to be another one of God's chosen mouthpieces.

To be deeply embedded in the things of God constitutes a hungry heart, a heart that is not concerned with the thoughts of men. Finney found himself on the verge of a life revolution. The things of God seemed to swell within him as if he would burst. To choose God would require laying down his own life, being oblivious to the opinions of men. Here, Finney found himself struggling with his faith in God. Yes, he believed the things of God, but to display it openly was not something he could so readily do. "I was shy, and avoided, as much as I could, speaking to anybody on the subject. I endeavored, however, to do this in a way, that would excite no suspicion, in any mind, that I was seeking the salvation of my soul,"[19] stated Finney. Yet the Spirit drew Him. Consumed with God and the thought of his own soul, he was brought to his face and cried out, "What, such a degraded sinner I am, on my knees confessing my sins to the great and holy God; and ashamed to have any human being, and a sinner like myself, find me on my knees endeavoring to make my peace with my offended God!"[20]

The sin broke him, to the point that any appearance of shame turned its ugly head. One encounter. One touch is all it took. The revolution began. Finney opened his heart and the adventure burst forth. With unscaled eyes, an open heart, and a mind aligned with Christ, Finney was awakened. He was shaken—shaken to the point of not recognizing his own nature. "It seemed as if my heart was all liquid."[21]

As a state of matter, liquid takes the shape of any vessel it is poured into. For Finney the vessel was full, or so he thought. Yet God was not finished. Finney once again encountered God in a way that would continue to burn a road of passion and influence the rest of his life. It was the baptism of the Holy Spirit.

> *But as I turned and was about to take a seat by the fire, I received a mighty baptism of the Holy Ghost. Without any expectation of it, without ever having the thought in my mind that there was any such thing for me, without any recollection that I had ever heard the thing mentioned by any person in the world, the Holy Spirit descended upon me in a manner that seemed to go through me, body and soul. I could feel the impression, like a wave of electricity, going through and through me. Indeed it seemed to come in waves and waves of liquid love, for I could not express it in any other way. It seemed like the very breath of God. I can recollect distinctly that it seemed to fan me, like immense wings.* [22]

Jeremiah 29:13 says, "You will seek Me and find Me when you seek Me with all your heart." Charles Finney sought and found. He didn't seek and give up. He battled, endeavored, and fought to break through the restlessness of his soul. He sought with his all and thus found an incomprehensible peace that surpassed even his own understanding. In finding, he rejoiced. For in finding appeared the greatest treasure of all, which he could not contain in his own soul.

EVAN ROBERTS

Evan Roberts was a revivalist in the early 1900s who was so compelled to see revival in Wales that he spent 11 years on his face weeping and praying for his nation. He walked in humility, and God readily turned His heart toward this young man of 26. In Second Chronicles 7:14-15 the Lord says,

*If My people, who are called by My name, will **humble themselves and pray and seek My face and turn from their wicked ways,** then will I hear from heaven and will forgive their sin and will heal their land. Now My eyes will be open and My ears attentive to the prayers offered in this place* (emphasis added).

Through the humbleness of Roberts and others of the 20th century, and through endless hours of prayer into the night and early morning, revival was sprung. The Lord was attentive to the prayers of His children, and Wales was drawn into an hour of repentance. The revival became so enhanced that city officials, businessmen, and news journalists came out of their workplace to experience this heavenly encounter. What once drew the people to enjoy random festivities no longer had its hold. Something new captured their attention. It was the same thing that drew Roberts to his room to pray when others his age would be engaged in outdoor activities. It was the thing that kept his heart captivated for hours between him and his God. The Holy Spirit began His work in this individual, and it could not be contained in his heart. Thus it burst forth and had the same affect on those willing to hear.

Whether it was by curiosity or genuine desire to be touched, no one left Roberts' meetings without being shaken by the supernatural. Interestingly, people were not drawn to the eloquence of his preaching, but to Roberts' sincere heart and desire to completely surrender the meetings over to the Holy Spirit's leading. Many times, praise and worship reverberated as people sang their praises to the Lord. And at other times, all was silent as God's Spirit moved among the hearts of sinners and saved alike. While Roberts spoke, the Holy Spirit fell. Meetings were said to extend until four o'clock in the morning, and even then, some people were still dispersed throughout the church. It was an hour of true repentance and heart searching. One journalist recalls his own experience while attending one of the revival services:

During the whole of this time the congregation was under the influence of deep religious fervour and exaltation. There were about 400 people present in the chapel when I took my seat at about nine o'clock…I had not been many minutes in the building before I felt that this was no ordinary gathering. Instead of the set order of proceedings to which we were accustomed at the orthodox religious service, everything here was left to the spontaneous impulse of the moment.

The journalist also noted,

A young woman rose to give out a hymn which was sung with deep earnestness. While it was being sung several people dropped down from their seats as if they had been struck and commenced crying for pardon. At 2.30 o'clock I took a rough note of what was then proceeding. In the gallery a woman was praying and she fainted. Water was offered her, but she refused this, saying the only thing she wanted was God's forgiveness. [23]

The desperation is clearly evident. This woman wanted nothing to satisfy the physical, but longed for what could only satisfy the depth of her soul. What a picture is drawn here with the journalist's words. And even words cannot adequately express a move of God, for it is more than one can fathom. When you are desperate for God as much as you are desperate for air, the miraculous transpires.

VESSELS NEEDED TODAY

Studying great men like Evan Roberts births an excitement in my own soul as I see God doing the same thing even today. Throughout our own various meetings, we have seen some of the very things that took place in the revivals that once spread throughout Wales. Often there are people so engaged in worship and so drawn into the presence of God that they have no desire to leave the services. Time no longer becomes a factor. Whether it is 11:00 PM or 1:00 AM has no importance. People are longing for more and are pressing in. When a service is given over to what God wants to do, and man is out of the way, the Holy Spirit is free to conduct the service and move in whatever way He chooses. The Holy Spirit will not be quenched.

May God and God alone be glorified through every meeting and every man be brought low, where only God is the focal point. God is always doing something new. He has no routine, and will often use different instruments and various methods to flow through, at different times of the service. There is no human structure involved, just divine order. We believe we are seeing another Welsh revival coming to America. Evan Roberts was a simple man who did not want to conform in any way, shape, or form to the religious system. He realized his nation needed the Almighty, and he was determined to do anything to see that Hand come down. May God wake up such men in America.

Chapter Eleven

ANOTHER
REFORMATION IS COMING

What was it about these men that God would set them apart? What caused them to surrender their all for the sake of the gospel? What set them on their course to reach thousands for Christ and gave them a relentless passion to proclaim God to every soul they came across? What was it that made these men redirect their own occupational objectives and careers to spread a message to the young and old alike? Perhaps it was a simple shakening that began within their own souls, a shakening that began as a gentle rumble and then expanded to a violent upheaval. In any case, these men were shaken to the core and wanted others to experience the same.

Merriam Webster's Dictionary defines *shaking* as "to move irregularly to and fro, to vibrate especially as the result of a blow or shock, to tremble as a result of physical or emotional disturbance, to experience a state of instability, or to briskly move something to and fro or up and down in order to mix."[24] These men were undeniably shaken. They were moved from a state of stagnancy to a place where they were blown away in the presence of God—from a place of being self-sufficient to a place of being unstable without God. They were moved from a place of mediocrity to a place of trembling before the Almighty. These men were available and willing vessels. They were vessels such as you and me. Smith Wigglesworth believed that every person who is a child of God could hold the power for the miraculous. He once stated, "Anyone can be ordinary, but a person filled with the Holy Spirit must be extraordinary."[25] Extraordinary is what Wigglesworth, Finney, Whitefield, Edwards, Roberts, Luther, and Wesley were. They ran after God with their whole being until the things of God were so engrained in them that it totally transformed them.

SHAKING THE PRISON DOORS OPEN AND THE CHAINS LOOSE

In God's Word we see another type of shaking. Although it took place in a natural sense, the supernatural was also alive and present.

> *About midnight Paul and Silas were praying and singing hymns to God, and the other prisoners were listening to them. Suddenly there was such a violent earthquake that the foundations of the prison were shaken. At once all the prison doors flew open, and everybody's chains came loose. The jailer woke up, and when he saw the prison doors open, he drew his sword and was about to kill himself because he thought the prisoners had escaped. But Paul shouted, "Don't harm yourself! We are all here!" The jailer called for lights, rushed in and fell trembling before Paul and Silas. He then brought them out and asked, "Sirs, what must I do to be saved?" They replied, "Believe in the Lord Jesus, and you will be saved—you and your household." Then they spoke the word of the Lord to him and to all the others in his house. At that hour of the night the jailer took them and washed their wounds; then immediately he and all his family were baptized. The jailer brought them into his house and set a meal before them; he was filled with joy because he had come to believe in God—he and his whole family (Acts 16:25-34).*

Be aware that the earthquake came in response to two direct acts—praying and singing. These two men were praying and singing before their God in the midst of a dark and dire situation. Praying and singing. Not crying and wailing. Praying and singing. They were doing this so much so, that the prisoners became attentive to their proclamations. Following this, the unexplainable took place. A shaking. An earthquake. A violent earthquake. An earthquake so violent that it shook the foundations. Could it be that through your praying, travailing, and worship as a follower of the Lord Jesus Christ, there can be a shaking among you?

This shaking that took place not only affected Paul and Silas, but also all those around them. Every single person in the vicinity of the jail felt the impact of the quake. Every door that was locked flew open; every chain that bound became loose. When there is a spiritual shaking, those in captivity and bondage are set free. Those who are oppressed gain a renewed vision. The hopeless become the hopeful.

In this story, the jailer, the head of the prison, couldn't help but be drawn to the chaos. Before Paul and Silas, he hit the ground trembling—trembling before these men of God. I believe it was a combination of natural fear mixed with a holy fear of God. In his heart of hearts, he asked the question we all have asked or must ask at one time or another, "What must I do to be saved?"

What prompted this life-embracing question? What made this man spill this question forth with such desperation? The jailer had an encounter that shook him. It caused him to delve deep into the resources of his own soul and to ponder what was in his heart. Anything and everything that was not of God was shaken from the recesses of his heart, and out came what mattered most. Through this encounter Paul and Silas replied, "Believe in the Lord Jesus." Not only did the jailer believe, but also his whole household. Notice the hour didn't matter. The jailer was ready. He had been shaken, and at the moment he was shaken, he desired the same for his family.

The time is now. It is time for the Church to be shaken out of its place. It is time to allow our own hearts to be stirred and awakened. I believe that America will be shaken in the same sort of way, and it will happen through uncompromised men who pay a price for the power and are not moved by what they see or feel. They will be individuals who press forth into the heavenly realms, and through this, the world will know and fear His name. The anointing will operate in and on us so mightily that multitudes will drop to their knees and ask, "What must I do to be saved?"

SHAKING THE HEAVENS, THE EARTH, AND THE NATIONS

The Scriptures also make it very clear that there will be another kind of shaking to come. Hebrews 12:26-29 states,

> At that time His voice shook the earth, but now He has promised, "Once more I will shake not only the earth but also the heavens." The words "once more" indicate the removing of what can be shaken—that is, created things— so that what cannot be shaken may remain. Therefore, since we are receiving a kingdom that cannot be shaken, let us be thankful, and so worship God acceptably with reverence and awe, for our "God is a consuming fire."

Haggai 2:6-7 also states,

> This is what the Lord Almighty says: "In a little while I will once more shake the heavens and the earth, the sea and the dry land. I will shake all nations, and the desired of all nations will come, and I will fill this house with glory," says the Lord Almighty.

The last-day Church must be ready for all that God desires to do in her and through her. For the Church to be prepared, I believe that God will shake her until she is spotless and right- eous without fault, having a vision for what God primarily intends the Church to be—a house of prayer.

Chapter Twelve

THE CRY
OF THE RIGHTEOUS

Every single move of God has been birthed while someone has been on their knees. In 1904 the nation of Wales experienced a spiritual revival because of the prayers of a young man named Evan Roberts.

Immediately before the power of God saturated the nation, it had been experiencing a major spiritual decline. Everything was taking place from public lewdness to outright immorality. The nation was filled with sin running rampant. People had completely strayed from God and were not attune to any morals or values whatsoever. Although the nation had been built on the principles of God-honoring and God-fearing men and women and they had once experienced great visitations from the Spirit of God, its condition had become deplorable, and a complacent attitude had engulfed the people. Disgusted by what he saw, Evan Roberts, at about the age of 26 began to pray. He, together with 17 teenagers, began to stand in the gap for their nation.[26]

THE TIRED FEW WHO WILL PRAY

America is in the same state today as Wales had been in 1904. Don't be blinded. The enemy is running rampant. Look at the way he has influenced normal everyday activities that can be viewed on the Internet or the TV screens in our own homes.

When you glimpse through the eyes of God, you will see what America really looks like today. Things are taking place, in every state and city that break the heart of God. You see it on the news, you hear about it from your coworkers, and read it in the paper. And these things are happening very close to you—closer than you think.

Have you heard of Mardi Gras in New Orleans, Louisiana? It is considered one of the largest party gatherings in the United States, a time where people get as immoral and crazy as they want right before the time of Lent. The most grotesque and sickest things you could ever conjure up in your mind take place there—things that are legal here in America! Have you been to Las Vegas or San Francisco? You better cover your eyes. Since 1950, our society has been drastically turned upside down. We need a revival now. We need an awakening now. And God is looking for a remnant who will pray. The revival that Wales experienced began with a handful of people praying on their knees. It wasn't hundreds or thousands. It was just a handful of people who prayed.

There is a fire burning in some hearts of people across America who are tired of the mundane and who are tired of the "same-old, same-old." They are weary of the religious slop. They are tired of the devil taking over their homes, schools, businesses, and governments. They are tired of the church structure as it is and seeing no move of the Holy Ghost. They are tired of reading and dreaming about revival. They don't just want to hear about revival; they want to experience it. They are tired, tired, tired.

REQUIREMENTS FOR REVIVAL

Before the awakening happened in Wales, God spoke very clearly to Evan Roberts and instructed him to do four things in order to see revival. First and foremost, people needed to begin to confess every known sin, and become right and holy before God. Whether it was outright, blatant sin or hidden sins of the heart, they needed to confess their wrong-doings and repent.

Second, people were to confess every unknown sin. Unknown sins are exactly that. They are sins that you are unaware that you have committed. One sin may even be that of religion. Religion can keep people in bondage! The most religious people don't even know that they are religious. The most bound don't even know that they are bound. Sometimes you don't know how bound you've been until you are set free.

Third, people were to meet daily and cry out. How badly do we want our nation to turn back to God? If you want something enough, you will pursue it. The proof of desire is in the pursuit.

I used to think I could pray, but I've come to find that I haven't understood what prayer really is. There were times when I first started my prayer life when I thought I would be praying for hours, only to find myself looking at my watch after only three minutes had passed. I used to pray for everything I could think of. Then I would look at my watch again and find that only seven minutes had passed. You see, the spirit is willing, but the flesh is weak. I believe there is an anointing to pray. The Spirit of God can come down and move you into places in prayer where you keep on praying, and the floodgates eventually open. It is a place where you find yourself not only praying for minutes, but for hours.

In the natural, a man can watch Saturday football for hours. One game starts at noon and before you know it, you're lost in the game and it is ten or eleven o'clock at night. The same thing can happen with movies. A double feature comes on and all at once you realize you have been sitting there for hours thinking, *Where did the time go?* If you can get lost like that in the natural, you can do that as well in the spiritual. It is a matter of training your flesh. Before a man stretches out for a whole-day marathon of football, he starts by watching just one game a weekend. Then one game becomes two games, which becomes three, and so on. Soon, he comes to the place where he really doesn't care who wins, but simply enjoys whatever is being broadcast. You can become that way with God too. It is a place where you stretch yourself out and get lost in the realms of God.

Fourth, the people of Wales were to take what they received, and give it out. The concept and logic is very simple. Go to God, cry out, go out, and give out. Cry out, go out, and give out. Say it over and over again. Cry out, go out, and give out. I hope and pray that as you read this, a hunger is being birthed in you. May you be that vessel that cries out to God, goes out to others, and gives out what God has given you. I pray that wherever you allow Him to take you that the fire of God rests all over you. Lord, revive us! Revive me!

THE CRY OF JESUS

Jesus knew that prayer was essential, and we should realize the same. In the garden of Gethsemane Jesus cried out to God, surrendering His life and giving over His will. Jesus prayed, "Not My will, but Your will be done."

Let's look at Scriptures where Jesus was moved to pray at this critical midnight hour:

> *And He came out, and went, as He was wont, to the mount of Olives; and His disciples also followed Him. And when He was at the place, He said unto them, Pray that ye enter not into temptation. **And He was withdrawn from them about a stone's cast, and kneeled down, and prayed,** saying, Father, if Thou be willing remove this cup from Me: nevertheless, not My will, but Thine, be done. And there appeared an angel unto Him from heaven, strengthening Him. **And being in an agony He prayed more earnestly:** and His sweat was as it were great drops of blood falling down to the ground. And when He rose up from prayer, and was come to His disciples, He found them sleeping for sorrow, and He said unto them, Why sleep ye? Rise and pray, lest ye enter into temptation* (Luke 22:39-46 KJV, emphasis added).

Reading in the Book of Matthew, we see the same incident taking place:

*Then saith He unto them, My soul is exceeding sorrowful, even unto death: tarry ye here, and watch with Me. **And He went a little farther, and fell on His face, and prayed,** saying, O My Father, if it be possible, let this cup pass from Me: nevertheless not as I will, but as Thou wilt. And He cometh unto the disciples, and findeth them asleep, and saith unto Peter, What, could ye not watch with Me one hour? Watch and pray, that ye enter not into temptation: the spirit indeed is willing, but the flesh is weak. He went away again the second time, and prayed, saying, O My Father, if this cup may not pass away from Me, except I drink it, Thy will be done. And He came and found them asleep again: for their eyes were heavy. And He left them, and went away again, and prayed the third time, saying the same words. Then cometh He to His disciples, and saith unto them, Sleep on now, and take your rest: behold, the hour is at hand, and the Son of man is betrayed into the hands of sinners. Rise, let us be going: behold, he is at hand that doth betray me* (Matt. 26:38-46 KJV, emphasis added).

Here was Jesus at His most critical hour, agonizing in prayer. I believe the most difficult time Jesus faced on earth took place in the garden of Gethsemane. The Lord didn't really die on the cross; He died in the garden. No man took His life; He laid it down. Everything became more and more of a reality. He knew it was here that He would have to give up His life. I believe that He always knew it was what He would do because He was God, but remember, He was also man. I believe it was here that it became a complete reality to Him.

There was something about Christ that seized the disciples' hearts. Maybe it was the distinct manner in which He lived His life, or His passion and the purpose for which He lived. Regardless, His life thoroughly transformed the lives of His disciples—a transformation that surged through them, soul and spirit, and convinced them to pursue the very thing that their Master and Savior Jesus died for.

CONVICTED TO CHANGE

And it came to pass, as we went to prayer, a certain damsel possessed with a spirit of divination met us, which brought her masters much gain by soothsaying: the same followed Paul and us, and cried, saying, These men are the servants of the most high God, which show unto us the way of salvation. And this did she many days, But Paul, being grieved, turned and said to the spirit, I command thee in the name of Jesus Christ to come out of her. And he came out the same hour. And when her masters saw that the hope of their gains was gone, they caught Paul and Silas, and drew them into the marketplace unto the rulers, and brought them to the magistrates, saying, These men, being Jews, do exceedingly trouble our city, and teach customs, which are not lawful for us to receive, neither to observe, being Romans. And the multitude rose up together against them: and the magistrates rent off their clothes, and commanded to beat them (Acts 16:16-22 KJV).

The early church was burdened and troubled for the world. Throughout Jesus' ministry, their eyes had been opened. Of all people, they knew the difference that Christ could make in any one person's life, and they wanted to make sure the world knew this. Their proclamations made their allegiances known as they entered city upon city, often turning them upside down. But not everyone was happy with the changes. When a move of God comes, many people will not understand what is happening. Others will be downright upset and angry. There have been times that we as a ministry have been criticized by others who are against any new move of God. We have even received death threats from the board members of a church. Revival will stir things up! A genuine move of the Holy Spirit brings sins to the surface; nothing is apt to remain hidden.

One of the jobs of the Holy Ghost is to bring conviction, and it is in that place of conviction where He draws the evil out of our lives and brings it to our attention. The Holy Ghost is holy! In a true move of God you can't remain in sin. You can't stay in adultery; you can't stay in fornication; you can't continue to snort cocaine or drink alcohol. God will deal with you. He wants to cleanse you so that you can be used for His purposes. He wants you to fulfill all that He has for you on the earth. He wants you to move on to another level with Him.

PERSECUTED, YET UNMOVED

We are always growing and changing, and sometimes we may experience some pretty trying circumstances.

Paul and Silas had been living holy and righteous lives. They were men living out their callings and purposes on the earth, yet they discovered that serving God was not always a cakewalk. It was actually far from a cakewalk. If anyone knew what persecution was, these men did. In this passage of Acts, multitudes had risen up against them and beat them. After many stripes had been laid upon their backs, they found themselves in a prison locked in stocks.

> *And when they had laid many stripes upon them, they cast them into prison, charging the jailor to keep them safely: who, having received such a charge, thrust them into the inner prison, and made their feet fast in the stocks. And at midnight Paul and Silas prayed, and sang praises unto God: and the prisoners heard them* (Acts 16:23-25 KJV).

I don't know what comes to your mind when you think of prison, but in this case, think of the worst. Paul and Silas were jammed into an inner prison, where the worst of the worst were held in utterly horrible surroundings. If anyone had a right to moan and complain, they did. But in the heat of the battle, in the midst of deplorable circumstances, they didn't complain—they praised. These men were what we call Christians. Absolutely nothing but Christ moved them. Too many Christians in the Body of Christ are moved by what they see and hear, by their emotions, thoughts, feelings, etc. But we are consider Paul and Silas as our examples—firmly grounded on the Rock.

John Wesley, a famous preacher of the 1700s, was saved on a ship traveling from England to America. While on board the ship, a storm arose. It was a storm so severe that everyone was preparing for the worst. As Wesley watched the waves beat against the sides of the boat, he began to evaluate His own heart. As a preacher, John Wesley thought he was saved, yet he had experienced no sense of peace. During the storm, fear overtook him and he frantically turned his head to find a group of Moravian people praying and worshipping God. Just as they were facing death, the Moravian people were having prayer and praise and worship time. As John Wesley watched them, something gripped his heart. These people had something right. It was at that moment that John Wesley was compelled to completely surrender his life to the Lord, and was saved. After seeing that nothing moved the Moravians from their faith, he knew he also wanted to live a life where nothing moved him. He realized that he had been living a life of religion, but he himself needed an awakening.[27]

It is in moments like these when you will discover how grounded your faith is and the depth of your trust in God. Paul and Silas were found worshiping and praising in the worst of circumstances. And their praise was very loud because it got the attention of the prisoners around them. Paul and Silas weren't whispering to God to help them. No. These men were bold; they were proclaiming their praises. While everyone was trying to sleep, they were worshiping and singing praises to Him!

A SHAKING, AN AWAKENING, AND AN ANSWER

Following this praise session, a great earthquake hit that city.

> *And suddenly there was a great earthquake, so that the foundations of the prison were **shaken**: and immediately all the doors were opened, and every one's bands were loosed* (Acts 16:26 KJV, emphasis added).

Through Scriptures God often speaks to us prophetically. The Old Testament stories actually happened, but they were also types and shadows of what was to come in the New Testament. In the same way, the New Testament stories are types and shadows of what is to happen in the future. I believe this story of Paul and Silas in prison is also a prophetic picture of the church praying and singing praises to God at the "midnight hour." We may be in our hour of agony, but I believe God will respond as He hears our midnight cries. Suddenly, there will be a great earthquake, an earthquake that not only shakes foundations but also wakes people out of their sleep. Our prayers have the power to shake places and bring about an awakening.

> And the keeper of the prison **awaking** out of his sleep, and seeing the prison doors open, he drew out his sword, and would have killed himself, supposing that the prisoners had been fled. But Paul cried with a loud voice, saying, "Do thyself no harm: for we are all here." Then he called for a light, and sprang in, and came trembling, and fell down before Paul and Silas, and brought them out, and said, **"Sirs, what must I do to be saved?"** And they said, "Believe on the Lord Jesus Christ, and thou shalt be saved, and thy house" (Acts 16:27-31 KJV, emphasis added).

When God hears our cries, the world will be shakened and awakened; and consequently, they will ask, "What must I do to be saved?" And we will respond, "Believe on the Lord Jesus Christ and you will be saved."

I believe that in this last day and hour, there will be a trembling anointing, and it will start from the cries of the righteous. The cries sent out at midnight will be the cries released from individuals all over America. It will be cries that take place not only in difficult circumstances but in everyday life. We need more all-night prayer meetings. We need people dedicated to prayer. Churches need to pray!

A PURSUIT OF TRAVAIL

There is an intimacy with the Father that comes only through the realm of prayer. He wants you to ascend to a realm of prayer that you have never been before. The Bible says that the righteous cry and the Lord hears. The Lord not only hears, but He delivers them from all their troubles. The reason He hasn't delivered us is because He hasn't heard us. The reason He hasn't heard us is because we are not crying out to Him. The proof of our desire is in the pursuit.

Many people *dream* about success, and then you have others who *pursue* or work hard for success. Take, for example, Tiger Woods. He is a great golfer, but he didn't just step out of his mother's womb and start swinging a club and putting a golf ball. On the contrary, he has worked hard as a superior athlete. And after he wins a championship, do you know where he goes? He returns to the practice tee and starts driving balls again. If men can have that kind of drive in the natural, there can also be that kind of drive or pursuit in the supernatural. Isaiah talks about a specific kind of drive in the supernatural called travailing.

> *Before she travailed, she brought forth; before her pain came, she was delivered of a man child. Who hath heard such a thing? Who hath seen such things? Shall the earth be made to bring forth in one day? Or shall a nation be born at once?* ***For as soon as Zion travailed, she brought forth her children*** (Isa. 66:7-8 KJV, emphasis added).

As soon as Zion travailed, she brought forth her children. Zion is the church. God says that *as soon* as we travail, children will be brought forth. In other words, as soon as the church decides to get serious, she will bring forth revival. God loves us. He loves us so much He sent His Son for us. He does not want one to perish, but all to have eternal life with HIM! The Bible calls sinners lost. Anything that is presently lost at one time can be found. When you see the guy sniffing cocaine on the streets, the teenager shooting up heroine, or the drunk guzzling his alcohol, you are looking at one of God's lost children. And when you look at them as a child of God, you will pursue them with more passion, for God is not willing that any of them should perish.

If you are a parent with multiple children, you know that each one of them is special to you. If you lost one, you wouldn't say, "That's all right. I have a couple left." You are not willing to lose any of your kids. Neither is God willing that any of His children should perish. When the church is likewise not willing that any should perish, we will have revival.

THE HOUR OF LABOR HAS COME

*Verily, verily, I say unto you, That ye shall weep and lament, but the world shall rejoice: and ye shall be sorrowful, but **your sorrow shall be turned into joy**. A woman when she is in travail hath sorrow, because her hour is come: **but as soon as** she is delivered of the child, she remembereth no more the anguish, for joy that a man is born into the world* (John 16:20-21 KJV, emphasis added).

Isn't it unique how God uses the birthing process to describe revival? God often speaks in ways to bring us to a fuller understanding of Him. I believe the church has been in a great process similar to that of a woman preparing to give birth. We have already gone through the three trimesters, or what we would call the nine months of pregnancy. The time of preparation has already taken place. The only stage yet to occur is the actual birthing, or what is called *labor*. Isn't it interesting that we would call it "labor"? The word *labor* means to work. In God's Word we are reminded that the harvest is plenty, but the laborers are few. Church, the children are ready to be birthed, but the ones willing to endure the labor are few.

I believe the church is presently in the darkest hour just before dawn, just as a woman faces her darkest hour before her baby is born. There is about to be the birthing of a new day, and in that new day we need to be persistent. If we want our families, schools, and America back, the church needs to wake up, get down on its knees, and cry out for revival! But until the church realizes the need, we won't see a move. The church must serve Him before the world will serve Him. Yes, it will be agony; yes it will be anguish, but it will be worth it. He is worth it.

Chapter Thirteen

WE NEED BREAD!

And it came to pass, that, as He was praying in a certain place, when He ceased, one of His disciples said unto Him, Lord, teach us to pray, as John also taught his disciples. And He said unto them, When ye pray, say, Our Father which art in heaven, Hallowed be thy name. Thy kingdom come. Thy will be done, as in heaven, so in earth. Give us day by day our daily bread. And forgive us our sins; for we also forgive every one that is indebted to us. And lead us not into temptation; but deliver us from evil. And He said unto them, Which of you shall have a friend, and shall go unto him at midnight, and say unto him, Friend, lend me three loaves; for a friend of mine in his journey is come to me, and I have nothing to set before him? And he from within shall answer and say, Trouble me not: the door is now shut, and my children are with me in bed; I cannot rise and give thee. I say unto you, Though he will not rise and give him, because he is his friend, yet because of his importunity he will rise and give him as many as he needeth. And I say unto you, Ask, and it shall be given you; seek, and ye shall find; knock, and it shall be opened unto you. For every one that asketh receiveth; and he that seeketh findeth; and to him that knocketh it shall be opened. If a son shall ask bread of any of you that is a father, will he give him a stone? Or if he asks a fish, will he for a fish give him a serpent? Or if he shall ask an egg, will he offer him a scorpion? If ye then,

*being evil, know how to give good gifts unto your children:
how much more shall your heavenly Father give the Holy
Spirit to them that ask Him?* (Luke 11:1-13 KJV).

There was something in the ministry of Jesus' prayer life
that caught the disciples' attention—something that inspired
them to come to Christ and say, "Teach us to pray like that!"

Jesus prayed with passion. I believe He knew exactly how
to approach His own Father. I don't believe He said things in
monotonous repetition. I believe He prayed with everything
inside Him, "Our Father!" Jesus was intense when He prayed.
Consider the prayer of Jesus in the garden of Gethsemane—He
was drenched in His own agonizing tears and sweat that was
like blood. He was well-acquainted with the psalms of David
where he passionately cried out to his Father, "Hear my cry
Lord; hear the cries of your people. Hear our cries!" And Jesus
prayed often in seclusion, developing an intimacy with the
Father. Several times in the Word we see that Jesus went off to
a private place to pray.

SHAMELESS PERSISTENCE

Immediately after Jesus taught the disciples how to pray, He
related a story about a man who came to his friend's house at
midnight, asking for some bread. Although it is very uncommon
to knock on someone's door so late at night, this man was determined to get some bread and began to knock on his neighbor's
door. Upon hearing the knocks, the master of the house yelled
from his bed, "Don't bother me now. My children are with me,
and we are sleeping!" The man at the door didn't give up. "I need
some bread; we have some visitors." Can you imagine the
response of the master of the house? "What!?" Then the request
comes again, "I need bread!" In the master's mind, and possibly
on his tongue are, "Hello buddy; it's midnight. Go away. Come
back another day!"

How would you expect the man who was begging for bread
to respond? How would you have responded? This man in his
determination began to knock again. His friend probably yelled

out the window, "What do you want now?" And again he shouted, "We need some bread!" The master of the house in irritation then said, "Go away. You are waking everybody up. Go away I said. Go away!" A few seconds passed, and there was once again a pounding on the door. "What!? I told you to go away." "I need some bread, you are my friend." "Go away!" "We need bread, please; we have got to have it now."

This man was insistent. He knew what he needed. And he kept knocking and knocking and knocking some more. The man in bed was definitely wide-awake now and most likely, less-than-kind thoughts were pouring rapidly through his mind concerning his friend—thoughts like, *This man is disturbed, maybe mentally disturbed. This guy is not going away. He doesn't have a clue. I could play this game all night; or I could give him some bread, tell him to hit the road, and everyone can get back to sleep.*

So the man acts. He doesn't decide to give him bread because he is a friend. He doesn't give him what he wants because of their relationship. But because of what the Bible calls "importunity"—shameless persistence—he rises and gives him what he has asked for. Likewise, God doesn't give to us because He owes us something. He acts because of our continual knocking.

Another important note is that the man at the door did not persist in order to accommodate himself. The bread was for his guests. The man sought so that he could give. His act was unselfish. He cried out for bread because he wanted to give it away. It is not about what God can do for us! It is about what we can do for God and for the people He places in our lives. It is up to you to be obedient. You are blessed to be a blessing. You are given to, so that you may give out.

BECAUSE THEY CRY NIGHT AND DAY

Jesus said regarding the Holy Spirit, "Ask and you will receive, seek and you will find, knock and it shall be opened unto you." When we ask, seek, and knock on the door for an outpouring of His Holy Spirit, God says that the door will be opened.

*And He spake a parable unto them to this end, that men ought always to pray, and **not to faint;** saying, There was in a city a judge, which feared not God, neither regarded man: and there was a widow in that city; and she came unto him, saying, Avenge me of mine adversary. And he would not for a while: but afterward he said within himself, Though I fear not God, nor regard man; yet because this widow troubleth me, I will avenge her, lest by her continual coming she weary me. And the Lord said, Hear what the unjust judge saith. And shall not God avenge His own elect, **which cry day and night** unto Him, though He bear long with them? I tell you that He will avenge them speedily. Nevertheless, when the Son of man cometh, shall He find faith on the earth?* (Luke 18:1-8 KJV, emphasis added).

Notice the words, "not to faint." Why did He teach not to faint? He knew that many people would faint. Why did Jesus say not to grow weary in well doing? He knew that we would grow weary.

However, God listens to those who cry out day and night, day and night, day and night—"We need bread, we need bread, we need bread." Here is a picture of what it means to travail. I once heard it said that we need less organizers in the church and more agonizers. We need a lot less say-ers, and a lot more prayers.

The Welsh Revival happened as a result of prayers that were like incense to God both day and night. Any revival is birthed through prayer. Consider the nation of Korea, which has been totally swept by God. There are over 100,000 people in each of three churches. Interestingly, that nation has not always been a Christian nation. Do you know how they came to that place? Prayer. They prayed all day and night. Being a Christian is not a tag they have; it is who they are. They just don't go to church; they are the Church.

In Africa people will come to services on their hands and knees. They will come through rainstorms to hear the life-saving message in Jesus Christ. The nation of Nigeria, more than any nation on the whole earth, has also been swept by God's hand. At a recent crusade with Reinhard Bonnke, there were approximately four million saved. They are now believing for ten million to get saved. One of the top pastors in that country was even raised from the dead! Church, God moves wherever there are hungry people.

The revival in Pensacola, Florida also came because people cried out for years. While having our revival in New Jersey we saw over 6,000 conversions, where people replaced that void with a relationship with Jesus. We were there for over three months and during that time, we saw people drive in from everywhere just to get a taste of heaven. The same kind of response took place in Michigan. We were there for over a year, and the revival lasted for close to six months. While there, we saw 11,000 people get saved. As we cried out and cried out, the Spirit of God filled that place. One of the top church leaders, who was 67 years old, approached me crying his eyes out, saying that he had been praying for a move like that for the last 25 years.

Who's Waiting on Whom?

I have prayed and asked the Lord, "When? When? When? When will we see revival?" Then I heard the Lord respond to me very clearly and say, "When? When? When?" God has been asking this same question much longer than we have. We have assumed that we've been waiting on God for an end-time revival, but He has been waiting on us. He has been waiting for the Ezekiels to speak life to the bones. We can have revival any time we want it. The Lord said wherever the soles of our feet tread is ours. Have we taken the land yet? As soon as Zion travails, God tells us He will avenge us speedily. We must keep knocking. We need bread!

Chapter Fourteen

OPEN YOUR EYES
AND SEE THE HARVEST

CAN YOU SEE THE HARVEST FIELD?

*"My food," said Jesus, "is to do the will of Him who sent Me to finish His work. Do you not say, 'Four months more and then the harvest'? **I tell you, open your eyes and look at the fields! They are ripe for harvest.** Even now the reaper draws his wages, even now he harvests the crop for eternal life, so that the sower and the reaper may be glad together"* (John 4:34-36, emphasis added).

As God's entrusted vessels, we must choose to open our eyes and look out to the fields that are already white unto harvest. We must look out and see as Jesus sees, not through the eyes of the flesh, but through the eyes of the Spirit. First Corinthians 2:12 states that as His beloved children, "we have not received the spirit of the world but the Spirit who is from God" (see also verses 10-11). Indwelt with the Spirit of God in these earthen vessels of ours, we have the ability to not only see through the natural but to see as He sees.

Where you are right now is not an accident, nor are the people you associate with. You have been assigned your job for a reason, and your city needs you. In the natural mind, you might consider yourself living a mundane life in an ordinary town with common people. If so, that is where your vision is skewed. There is more that surrounds you than you realize. There is always more going on than your natural mind can conceive.

Stand still for one moment in your workplace. Pause and look at those around you. You are not looking at just people. You are not just doing the mundane. No. You are standing in a harvest field. All around you are unharvested fields and you have been equipped with the tools necessary to gather the harvest. Your heavenly Father has commissioned you to be a part of this harvest. Whether you are a sower or a reaper, you have an appointed position. However, we must change our perspective; we must see the world the way Jesus sees it.

THE EYEGLASSES OF ETERNITY

We must put on a new set of eyeglasses so that we can see supernaturally. Looking through the eyeglasses of eternity you will see events, not just as ordinary, but as life encounters, divine appointments, and God-given opportunities to bring in the harvest. Looking through these lenses, you will once again realize what Jesus did for you, and you will want others to experience Him for who He is. The world and its purpose will once again come into focus. In Hebrews 13:5-6 we read,

> God has said, "Never will I leave you; never will I forsake you." So we say with confidence, "The Lord is my helper; I will not be afraid. What can man do to me?"

"What can man do to me?" The answer is…nothing. The real question is, "What can I do for man?"

We all are aware of the condition of our world. Even when we turn on the news for a few minutes, we see everything from the hurting to the hopeless to the needy to the lost. Billboards set along highways advertise help for those who are finding it hard to cope with their situations. Christian networks have established hope-lines for people to call in for prayer. Advertisements flash up on the television screen asking for financial support for children who are starving in third world countries. The needs extend all over the world, to every one of the seven continents. We are a needy people, and we have a dire need for a Savior.

John 3:16-17 says, "For God so loved the world, that He gave His only begotten Son, that whosoever believeth in Him should not perish, but have everlasting life. For God sent not His Son into the world to condemn the world; but that the world through Him might be saved." For God so loved the world that He gave. Jesus gave His all; He gave His life. Jesus was compelled to draw people to Himself and thus to give His life for us. In giving His life He became the Savior of the world. We must do the same and look out into the world and realize the need of a Savior. The Lord does not want any one person to perish, but desires that everyone come to repentance. For a person to come to repentance, he must hear the truth; and it is our responsibility to spread this message. This same desire that compelled the heart of God to give His only Son for us so that none would perish must also ring true in our hearts. The desire and desperation to see that no one perishes comes with recognizing that the harvest is white and ready.

GETTING READY FOR THE HARVEST

God is preparing us now for His last-days work. We need to be ready for a great harvest, and to get ready for that harvest, we must work. God needs laborers.

*And He said unto them, **Go** ye into all the world, and preach the gospel to every creature. He that believeth and is baptized shall be saved; but he that believeth not shall be damned. And these signs shall follow them that believe; in My name shall they cast out devils; they shall speak with new tongues; they shall take up serpents; and if they drink any deadly thing, it shall not hurt them; they shall lay hands on the sick, and they shall recover. So then after the Lord had spoken unto them, He was received up into heaven, and sat on the right hand of God. **And they went forth, and preached everywhere,** the Lord working with*

them, and confirming the word with signs following. Amen
(Mark 16:15-20 KJV, emphasis added)

The disciples went forth and preached everywhere—everywhere! Jesus told them to go into all the world and preach the gospel to every creature.

JUST GO!

What Christians need to hear is *go!* Jesus was always telling His disciples to go! Go! He never said to sit still and wait for sinners to come. He said to *go*. Many times we try to second-guess God. Often we sit and wonder what God has for us and what He wants us to do. But have you ever thought that just maybe it is time to *go?*

Go is a verb. It is an action word. *Go* means doing! You can *go* to the mission field or you can *go* to the supermarket. Some people are called to those uttermost places of the earth, while some are called to "Judea," or to go to their own "Jerusalem." Some people erroneously think that "full-time" ministers are supposed to go, while all others are to stay. But, in fact, every one of us is in full-time ministry for the Lord, no matter our occupation. You are a vessel and God is determined to use you. Simply make yourself willing and open.

Jesus Himself was very transient and always on the move. Even though many times people tried to stop Jesus and convince Him to build a tabernacle or stay at a certain place, He said, "No, I have to go." Jesus knew His calling and made sure He spread the message to everyone He met.

GO AND PREACH

When we finally do realize that God wants us to go, what should we do when we go? We are to preach. To preach basically means to open your mouth and say something. Preaching is declaring. Preaching does not mean teaching. Preaching is proclaiming. It is making a proclamation.

Preach. Say something. Tell the world. God wants to use our mouths. He is looking for the church's voice. The church has had a voice to itself for too long. We talk a lot; but when we talk, we talk to each other, prophesy over each other, or exhort one another—and only inside the building. I believe that God wants to use our mouths outside the building. We need a vocal church in the public ear. We need a church endued with the power of God, a church anointed with the fire of God, preaching and saying something outside the building. People need to use their voices outside for God just as Jesus spent much of His life outside the "church."

PREACH THE GOOD NEWS

Now that you know you are to go, and now that you know you are to preach, you might wonder, *What do I preach?* You preach the gospel. Go into the world and preach the gospel—in Jerusalem, Judea, Samaria, and to the uttermost parts of the earth (see Acts 1:8). Don't preach your own convictions. Preach the solid gospel—simply proclaim Him! Actually, the church already preaches a lot, but unfortunately, not much of it is the gospel. Go preach the gospel into the entire world. The gospel sets people free! Tell people God loves them; He died for them; and He is alive now and has a purpose for them. Proclaim the gospel, the good news.

Sometimes we start an intellectual conversation with someone that soon turns into an argument or debate. However, Jesus never said to do that. The gospel is not to be argued. We are to preach and proclaim. I don't ever argue the gospel. I proclaim the gospel. Paul said, "I am not ashamed of the gospel, for it is the power of God." The gospel proclaims its power. The gospel is inarguable. It is 100 percent infallible. Our job is not to convince people that Jesus is Lord. We don't need to convince anyone. Jesus Christ is Lord whether people believe it or not. Just tell people how much God loves them and that He has a plan for them. There is something about the gospel and the name of Jesus that doesn't need to be argued. Just tell people about Him.

OPEN YOUR MOUTH

To proclaim the gospel is to open your mouth and speak. It is not laying a track on the back of a toilet or putting a flyer in a mailbox. I know through the ministry of tracks, many people have been saved. Tracks are a wonderful method for explaining the gospel, and I thank God for tracks; but I've personally decided to stop handing them out.

As a young man, I had made it my mission to hand out tracks to people I came into contact with or passed by, and I felt pretty good about the whole thing until I came across a man who "stopped me in my own tracks."

After handing him a track, I turned to walk away when he said, "What's this?" This man already had some sort of inclination as to what the track was as he sat there staring at it. I replied, "Read this, sir. It is very important. It is about life and death." He looked down at it again and then looked back at me and said, "Hold on, hold on." I paused wondering what he was going to say, hoping he would accept Jesus right there. Then he said, "You mean to tell me that this is what you believe? This is eternal life for me?" I said, "Yeah!" He said, "This is what you do with your life? You hand out these little booklets?" I said, "Yeah." He said, "This is the most important thing in life, right?" And I said, "Yes!" Little did I know that the next words that would come out of his mouth would change my life. "And you couldn't even stop to tell me about it? You couldn't open your mouth to tell me about something that is life-and-death important, but you can hand me a piece of paper? ...No thanks." And tossing the booklet in the air, he turned and walked away.

Track ministry is great, but most people who hand out tracks do so because they don't like confrontation. They'll distribute a thousand tracks, passing them out all over the place. And while some of them really make it into people's hands, others sprinkle the bathroom floor. If you are handing out tracks as a testimony, keep it up. You never know where they might land, but don't let them hinder you from opening your mouth. Let me make it very clear—the world is dying. Allow your own life to be a testimony. You are a living track. As Christians, we are a living witness, a living Bible so that all men can read. Ask the Lord to give you an opportunity to share the gospel; and then, when He brings that person across your path, say something. Open your mouth.

WHEN DO WE PREACH?

When do we preach? *Now!* We can't wait any longer. We can't put it off any longer. Now! Two thousand years ago Jesus said, "Look up, lift up your eyes, the fields are white." He went about the villages teaching, preaching, and healing. Moved with compassion because of the multitudes and the lost people, He said, "Pray and get on your knees that the Lord will send laborers." God wants laborers. Without laborers a harvest field cannot be harvested. Laborers are people who work. Labor requires sacrifice, a lot of time, and commitment. Will you be a laborer?

The church of Jesus Christ has such potential. Winning souls must become the utmost priority. Unfortunately, an estimated 98 percent of the church body has never led someone to Jesus Christ. A church that doesn't win the lost is not a church at all. During services, I watch God move, transforming lives right before my very eyes, and I see people fall out in the Spirit all the time, but that is not what charges me. What fires me up is when people get saved. Jesus had power, but that is not what consumed Him. He came to seek and save the lost. Along with our miracle services, we always provide an altar call so that people never come into a service without having the opportunity to accept Jesus Christ as their Savior. At these services the power of God is demonstrated for lost people. It is proof providing power.

Proof providing power provides proof to people who need proof. Do you need proof? I don't need proof. I believe Him. He said, "Blessed are those who don't have to see, yet still believe." Yet some people need to see. He didn't discredit them. He knew that some would only believe based on what they saw. And in seeing, they were moved.

A Christian who doesn't win the lost is not a Christian at all, because Jesus said, "If you follow Me, I will make you a fisher of men." It must be the very focus of your Christian walk. Jesus emphasized, "Freely you have received, now freely give." Freely you have received; freely He forgave you and did something for you, and freely you should go tell someone. Surely He should be worth telling. Surely you could tell somebody. We live in an urgent hour. He has chosen you and me for such a time. God is waiting on us for the greatest move that the planet earth has ever seen. Just as it happened for the disciples, it will likewise happen again when we go and spread the gospel to the lost today.

Today. Today is the day of salvation. Some people will never see tomorrow. It will be too late for them. God has placed particular people in your life for certain reasons, and it is up to you to tell them what you know. The only thing you will ever be able to take to heaven with you is another person you led to Christ. Although we know the devil is defeated, he will still try to convince you to keep your mouth shut. Be strong in the Lord. Open your mouth, for today—now—is the day of salvation.

Chapter Fifteen

LIGHT THE WORLD
WITH LOVE

Unto the angel of the church of Ephesus write; These things saith He that holdeth the seven stars in His right hand, who walketh in the midst of the seven golden candlesticks; I know thy works, and thy labor, and thy patience, and how thou canst not bear them which are evil: and thou hast tried them which say they are apostles, and are not, and hast found them liars: and hast borne, and hast patience, and for My name's sake hast labored, and hast not fainted. Nevertheless I have somewhat against thee, **because thou hast left thy first love.** *Remember therefore from whence thou art fallen, and repent, and* **do the first works;** *or else I will come unto thee quickly, and will* **remove thy candlestick** *out of his place, except thou repent. But this thou hast, that thou hatest the deeds of the Nicolaitans, which I also hate. He that hath an ear, let him hear what the Spirit saith unto the churches; to him that overcometh will I give to eat of the tree of life, which is in the midst of the paradise of God* (Rev. 2:1-7 KJV, emphasis added).

In this Scripture, Jesus distinctly addresses the church at Ephesus and for three verses, He basically pats them on the back for their diligence, perseverance, and good works. Then Jesus suddenly becomes quite blunt and very matter of fact. He has no time to play games. Their "crime" is a serious one.

Drastic changes need to be made. They have left their "first love" (see Rev. 2:4).

WHAT WAS THEIR "FIRST LOVE"?

For years, the intensity of this verse, Revelation 2:4, has stood out in my mind. I desired to know exactly what Christ meant when He said, "first love." So my research began. Because Jesus, in the Book of Revelation, was rebuking the church at Ephesus for leaving their first love, it would benefit us to know what their first love was.

As my research continued, I was led to the Book of Acts, specifically chapter 19 where the apostle Paul proceeded to stir up some disciples in the faith in the community of Ephesus. Reading this chapter, we are given some details concerning what the Ephesian church was first like. (And remember, the Word is living and active, and is for our present edification as well.)

> ...*Paul having passed through the upper coasts came to Ephesus....And he said unto them, Unto what then were ye baptized? And they said, Unto John's baptism. Then said Paul, John verily baptized with the baptism of repentance, saying unto the people, that they should believe on Him which should come after him, that is, on Christ Jesus. When they heard this, they were baptized in the name of the Lord Jesus. And when Paul had laid his hands upon them, the Holy Ghost came on them; and they spake with tongues, and prophesied. And all the men were about twelve. And he went into the synagogue, and spake boldly for the space of three months, disputing and persuading the things concerning the kingdom of God. But when divers were hardened, and believed not, but spake evil of that way before the multitude, he departed from them, and separated the disciples, disputing **daily** in the school of one Tyrannus. **And this continued by the space of two years; so that all they which dwelt in Asia heard the word of the Lord Jesus, both Jews and Greeks**** (Acts 19:1-10 KJV, emphasis added).

The Word of God says that the whole region of Asia heard the Word of the Lord Jesus, both Jews and Greeks. If the Word says it, then it is. Everyone heard! Everyone! This was a church that had a *passion for souls and a passion for the lost. That* was their first love.

> *And many that believed came, and confessed, and showed their deeds. Many of them also which used curious arts brought their books together, and burned them before all men: and they counted the price of them, and found it fifty thousand pieces of silver.* **So mightily grew the word of God and prevailed** (Acts 19:18-20 KJV, emphasis added).

Did you notice who it was who burned those books and used curious arts? They were sinners. And how did the sinners come to believe? Someone with a love for souls had to go to where they were at and tell them.

LOVE—THE GREATEST COMMANDMENT

This is the message you heard from the beginning: We should love one another (1 John 3:11).

C.S. Lewis stated, "Though our feelings come and go, His love for us does not. It is not wearied by our sins, or our indifference; and, therefore, it is quite relentless in its determination that we shall be cured of those sins, at whatever cost to us, at whatever cost to Him."[28]

From the beginning of time and the creation of the universe and man, we see nothing less than an expression of God's unfathomable love. Jesus Himself came to this earth as atonement for our sin and a sacrifice of love. Line after line, verse after verse, God's Word is filled with descriptions of God's abounding love.

> *The Lord, the Lord, the compassionate and gracious God, slow to anger,* **abounding in love** *and faithfulness, maintaining love to thousands, and forgiving wickedness, rebellion and sin* (Exod. 34:6, emphasis added).

Your love, O Lord, reaches to the heavens, Your faithfulness to the skies (Ps. 36:5, emphasis added).

Because your love is better than life, my lips will glorify You (Ps. 63:3, emphasis added).

For great is Your love toward me (Ps. 86:13a, emphasis added).

For as high as the heavens are above the earth, so great is His love for those who fear Him (Ps. 103:11, emphasis added).

Because of the Lord's great love we are not consumed, for His compassions never fail. They are new every morning; great is Your faithfulness (Lam. 3:22-23, emphasis added).

How great is the love the Father has lavished on us, that we should be called children of God! (1 John 3:1, emphasis added).

This is how we know what love is: Jesus Christ laid down His life for us (1 John 3:16-17, emphasis added).

We love because He first loved us (1 John 4:19).

Dear friends, let us love one another, for love comes from God. Everyone who loves has been born of God and knows God. Whoever does not love does not know God, because God is love. This is how God showed His love among us: He sent His one and only Son into the world that we might live through Him. This is love: not that we loved God, but that He loved us and sent His Son as an atoning sacrifice for our sins. Dear friends, since God so loved us, we also ought to love one another. No one has ever seen God; but if we love one another, God lives in us and His love is made complete in us (1 John 4:7-12, emphasis added).

You may ask what true Christianity is. It is love. We are, because He loved. We are, because He gave His life. Without His love we would have tasted death. And in receiving His love, we must also give His love.

You may consider yourself a great Christian. You go to church, you spend time in the Word, you pray for others and over others, and you tithe. You may be a pastor, a preacher, or a teacher. But suppose that what you do is not enough? It doesn't matter if it isn't enough for my standards. What if it isn't enough for His?

Ponder these words of the apostle Paul.

If I speak in the tongues of men and of angels, **but have not** **love,** *I am only a resounding gong or a clanging cymbal. If I have the gift of prophecy and can fathom all mysteries and all knowledge, and if I have a faith that can move mountains,* **but have not love,** *I am nothing. If I give all I possess to the poor and surrender my body to the flames,* **but have not love,** *I gain nothing* (1 Cor. 13:1-3, emphasis added).

Intense? Convicting? Heart searching? Read them again. Allow them to penetrate and pierce. The fact is simple. You are nothing, and you gain nothing…without love. This is not to bring fear but revelation to your heart. No matter what you do, if it is not done with of a heart of love, it is basically empty—meaningless. The key to life and knowing God to the fullest is having a love relationship with Him and pouring that same love onto others.

Smith Wigglesworth was a man who exhibited God's love and compassion in everything he did. In the book, *The Secret of His Power*, Albert Hibbert describes Wigglesworth as having no special technique for what he did; he was simply motivated by the love of God. He knew in his heart that techniques counted for nothing without love. Albert Hibbert states, "Love puts the best possible construction on any situation; it sees the potential for good in the very worst characters. For this reason, love succeeds when everything else fails. This love is what brought much success in Wigglesworth's ministry."[29] Wigglesworth could not do anything if it wasn't for the overwhelming compassion he felt for others. He had the Father's heart. Thus tears would flood his eyes many times when he saw those who were hurting, needy, or lost. Now if a man like Wigglesworth, who impacted thousands, knew that everything he did had to be a direct reflection of his love for others, don't you think we also ought to apply everything we do on the simple yet profound principal of love?

No Small Matter

*And the same time there arose no small stir about that way. For a certain man named Demetrius, a silversmith, which made silver shrines for Diana, brought no small gain unto the craftsmen; whom he called together with the workmen of like occupation, and said, Sirs, ye know that by this craft we have our wealth. Moreover ye see and hear, that not alone at Ephesus, **but almost throughout all Asia, this Paul hath persuaded and turned away much people, saying that they be no gods, which are made with hands:** so that not only this our craft is in danger to be set at nought; but also that the temple of the great goddess Diana should be despised, and her magnificence should be destroyed, whom all Asia and the world worshippeth. And when they heard these sayings, they were full of wrath, and cried out, saying, Great is Diana of the Ephesians. And the whole city was filled with confusion: and having caught Gaius and Aristarchus, men of Macedonia, Paul's companions in travel, they rushed with one accord into the theatre. And when Paul would have entered in unto the people, the disciples suffered him not....For we are in danger to be called in question for this day's uproar, there being no cause whereby we may give an account of this concourse....And after the uproar was ceased...* (Acts 19:23-30,40;20:1 KJV emphasis added).

The entire city of Ephesus was in an uproar. Actually this was not just an uproar; this was a riot. They were preaching the gospel in every nook and cranny. They invaded the whole town...everywhere. There were no limitations. They didn't care if they encroached upon the space of the "magical" people. They were going to where the lost needed to hear.

We know very little else about the church of Ephesus other than what you have just read. But most importantly we discover that there was a riot. I'm wondering—how many churches today are causing riots and uproars?

God has led me to prepare the church to be submerged into a state of evangelism. Having a "first love" is to exhibit an unmatched passion for the lost, and be seriously determined to share the gospel with others. It is moving people from their place in the pews, outside the doors, and onto the streets.

LET YOUR LIGHT SHINE

Jesus continued to admonish the church at Ephesus in Revelation 2:5:

Remember therefore from whence thou art fallen, and repent, **and do the first works;** *or else I will come unto thee quickly, and will remove thy candlestick out of his place, except thou repent* (KJV, emphasis added).

Jesus associated their "first works"—reaching out to people—with their "first love." This first love is mentioned in the Book of Matthew, when Jesus was asked about the greatest commandment. He responded with two answers: Love the Lord thy God with all thy heart, and with all thy soul, and with all thy mind...and love thy neighbor as thyself (Mt. 22:37,39). Jesus warned the Ephesians that if they neglected to love the Lord and their neighbors, He would remove their candlestick or their light.

Ye are the salt of the earth: but if the salt have lost his savor, wherewith shall it be salted? It is thenceforth good for nothing, but to be cast out, and to be trodden under foot of men. **Ye are the light of the world.** *A city that is set on an hill cannot be hid. Neither do men light a candle, and put it under a bushel, but on a candlestick; and it giveth light unto all that are in the house.* **Let your light** *so shine before men, that they may see your good works, and glorify your Father which is in heaven* (Matt. 5:13-16 KJV, emphasis added).

Throughout Scripture we are reminded that Jesus was and is the light of the world. He was very clear when He said, "I am the light of the world" (Jn. 8:12). On the other hand, this scripture in Matthew says, "Ye are the light of the world." So…He is the light of the world, and you are the light of the world. Which one is it? Actually, it is both. Why? The answer is quite simple: Our light is His light. Jesus lives on the inside of us. His light on the inside of us shines through to the outside.

In the beginning was the Word, and the Word was with God, and the Word was God. The same was in the beginning with God. All things were made by Him; and without Him was not any thing made that was made. In Him was life; and the life was the light of men. **And the light shineth in darkness; and the darkness comprehended it not.** *There was a man sent from God, whose name was John. The same came for a witness, to bear witness of the Light, that all men through Him might believe. He was not that Light, but was sent to bear witness of that Light* (John 1:1-8 KJV, emphasis added).

Here we have a scripture that justifies the purpose of the light. He lives in full measure on the inside of us. The light that shone so brightly on the face of the earth thousands of years ago continues to radiate through us. That light has the power and ability to penetrate the darkness of this world! That life of Jesus, being the light of men, lives on the inside of us enabling us to become the light of the world. Jesus becomes the light through us. Since that light dwells in us, it is our responsibility to take that light to others.

A LIGHT SHINES
BRIGHTER IN THE DARKNESS

When you enter a dark room and you turn on the light, the darkness disappears. The light comes in and radiates. When the light comes in and radiates, the darkness flees. Yes, it flees. Darkness has no power against light. So, if the light is stronger than darkness, we have nothing to fear. Therefore, if the church, who is inhabited by the light, enters a dark world, the darkness must be overcome by the light. What I have come to realize though, is that the church is trying to do everything they can to keep the light to themselves. We train in our Bible schools; we read the Word among ourselves; we have fellowship meetings inside our buildings; and actually what we are doing is enhancing our own lights. We are getting brighter and brighter simply by hanging out with other lights. And while the church is burning brighter, there is still a dark, lost world outside searching for the light.

Believers, the world is not *the* darkness; but it is *in* the darkness. The darkness is the enemy. In the darkness, thousands are living meaningless lives, looking for the light. Once they get a glimpse of light, they will run to it, because it is what they have been looking for. The gates of hell are a dark place, a very dark place. But how can people expect to see the light unless we shine it for them to see? Many lights are hiding in a place where they cannot be seen. They've been hiding under a bushel, but it is time for those lights to shine.

AMERICA NEEDS THE LIGHT TO SHINE

Jesus commended the church of Ephesus for some of their works, but rebuked them because they had lost their first love. They had once possessed a passion for people and had let their light shine.

As mentioned previously, 98 percent of Christians in the world have never led a person to Jesus Christ. Dr. James Kennedy once quoted a statistic, that in 1900, 964 people were daily coming to the Lord all around the world. In the year 2000, over 200,000 people were coming to Christ every day. But do you know where most of those people live? In other countries. Why? Their light is invading the darkness.

But now must be America's time. We have more lights than any nation on the earth. We have accomplished great things in the church, but we have lost our first love. This is the time for Jesus to shine in our world. We must take our light outside the four walls of the church; go and invade the very darkness of hell. This is exactly what God has called our ministry to do. The church is required to take their lights out into the darkness. Do not allow the devil's tactics of fear to entrap you and hold you back. Take note, the gates of hell cannot prevail against you. Even in the midst of the darkest places, a little light will shine.

Chapter Sixteen

THE WORKS OF GOD

*And as Jesus passed by, He saw a man which was blind from his birth. And His disciples asked Him, saying, Master, who did sin, this man, or his parents, that he was born blind? Jesus answered, Neither hath this man sinned, nor his parents: but that **the works of God should be made manifest in him.** I must work the works of Him that sent Me, while it is day: the night cometh, when no man can work. As long as I am in the world, I am the light of the world* (John 9:1-5 KJV, emphasis added).

*Philip saith unto Him, Lord, show us the Father, and it sufficeth us. Jesus saith unto him, Have I been so long time with you, and yet hast thou not known Me, Philip? He that hath seen Me hath seen the Father; and how sayest thou then, Show us the Father? Believest thou not that I am in the Father, and the Father in Me? The words that I speak unto you I speak not of Myself: but the Father that dwelleth in Me, **He doeth the works*** (John 14:8-10 KJV, emphasis added).

If you have seen Jesus, you have seen the Father. If you want to find out what the Father is like, then look at Jesus, because He was the Father in action. Jesus did the works of His Father. To know God's will, once again, look at Jesus. Why? Because He performed the Father's will.

GREATER WORKS WILL YOU DO

*Believe Me that **I am in the Father, and the Father in Me:***
***or else believe Me for the very works' sake**. Verily, verily, I*
*say unto you, He that believeth on Me, **the works** that I do*
*shall he do also; and **greater works** than these shall he do;*
because I go unto My Father. And whatsoever ye shall ask
in My name, that will I do, that the Father may be glorified
in the Son. If ye shall ask any thing in My name, I will do it
(John 14:11-14 KJV, emphasis added).

This Scripture text is based on the works of Jesus and the
manifesting power of God. Jesus said, "Believe Me...or else
believe Me because of the *works!*" Jesus said, "I must do the
works of Him who sent Me." While there is still light on this
earth, we have to work the works of God. Jesus said that those
people who believed in Him would do greater works than He
had done Himself. Doesn't that just blow you away? He is talking to every single one of us. You are to work the works of Jesus.

During the Good News New York Crusade, we along with
other churches were out fishing for souls, and over 48,000 people
came to Christ. Because we spoke words with our mouths, thousands were saved. Just think of how mind-boggling that is! What
is even more humbling, is that as vessels, we were not just speaking words, but we were empowered with the Holy Ghost. Jesus
didn't just send His disciples out with mere words; they went out
with the power of God.

> *And Jesus went about all the cities and villages, teaching in*
> *their synagogues, and preaching the gospel of the kingdom,*
> *and healing every sickness and every disease among the peo-*
> *ple. But when He saw the multitudes, He was moved with*
> *compassion on them, because they fainted, and were scat-*
> *tered abroad, as sheep having no shepherd. Then saith He*
> *unto His disciples, The harvest truly is plenteous, but the*
> *labourers are few; **pray ye therefore the Lord of the har-***
> ***vest, that He will send forth labourers into His harvest***
> *(Matt. 9:35-38 KJV, emphasis added).*

The Amplified Bible tells us to pray that the Lord of the harvest will force and thrust out laborers into His harvest. In calling His 12 disciples, He gave them power against unclean spirits and enabled them to heal all manner of sickness and diseases.

DON'T BE AFRAID TO GO AND GIVE

These 12 Jesus sent forth, and commanded them, saying, "Go not into the way of the Gentiles, and into any city of the Samaritans enter ye not: but go rather to the lost sheep of the house of Israel. And as ye go, preach, saying, The kingdom of heaven is at hand. Heal the sick, cleanse the lepers, raise the dead, cast out devils: freely ye have received, freely give....Behold, I send you forth as sheep in the midst of wolves: be ye therefore wise as serpents, and harmless as doves" (Matt. 10:5-8,16 KJV).

We are as sheep being sent out among the wolves. However, if it were up to the sheep, they would never approach a pack of wolves. It is a terrifying thought. Sheep would rather stay with other sheep. Other sheep aren't dangerous or threatening like wolves. Therefore, in order for a sheep to approach a wolf, he has to be empowered with something more than his very own nature. In order to walk confidently among the wolves, the sheep must know their shepherd is with them.

We must walk out with that same kind of confidence knowing that God has instilled something within us that is greater than that which is in the world. He has given us the power to do the same things He did. Jesus healed the sick, cleansed the leper, and raised the dead. He lives on the inside of you as a believer. Freely you have received, freely give.

It was once said that the key to revival is "obedience to God's Word." Obey the Word that says you shall lay your hands on the sick and they shall recover. Obey the Word that says to go into all the world and preach the gospel. Freely you have received, freely give.

Jesus sent His disciples out with power. That is what we are also expected to do—go out with power. Be bold. Lay your hands on one another. Pray in the name of Jesus Christ with boldness. Do you remember what happened when Jesus was at the well and the woman came to draw water? Jesus said only a few words to her. "Woman, you have five husbands." With one manifestation of the word of knowledge, the lady went back and won her entire town to Christ. Can you imagine what would happen in your town through one little miracle? Do we really believe the Bible? Do we believe we can do the same works? If we believe it, then our actions need to speak for it.

PEOPLE ARE WAITING FOR PROOF

Every day in courtrooms all over this nation, lawyers present cases before judges and juries—divorce cases, criminal cases, civil cases, and personal conflicts. The basis for deciding if someone is innocent or guilty is the evidence or proof that is provided. Proof determines if people spend time in jail, keep or lose their children, maintain or relinquish their goods to someone else. In our American criminal justice system, one is innocent until proven guilty. Even the worst criminals in our society have to be proven guilty before being sentenced. Proof is vital.

In the spiritual realm, proof is also vital. Even in the days when Moses and Aaron stood before Pharaoh, the world wanted proof. Exodus 7:8-13 (NIV) reads,

> The Lord said to Moses and Aaron, "When Pharaoh says to you, 'Perform a miracle,' then say to Aaron, 'Take your staff and throw it down before Pharaoh,' and it will become a snake." So Moses and Aaron went to Pharaoh and did just as the Lord commanded. Aaron threw his staff down in front of Pharaoh and his officials, and it became a snake. Pharaoh then summoned wise men and sorcerers, and the Egyptian magicians also did the same things by their secret arts: each one threw down his staff and it became a snake. But Aaron's staff swallowed up their staffs. Yet Pharaoh's

heart became hard and he would not listen to them, just as the Lord had said (Exod. 7:8-13).

The devil is not shy of his power. However, his power can never withstand God's power. Never. Aaron's staff/snake swallowed all the other staffs/snakes. God's power is genuine. In our society today though, many evil works are being demonstrated while the church sits back and shows little, if any, of God's works. Consequently, people are witnessing only the "rod of Pharaoh"— the works of the world.

THE WORKS WILL
SPEAK FOR THEMSELVES

*Now when John had heard in the prison the **works of Christ**, he sent two of his disciples, and said unto Him, Art Thou He that should come, or do we look for another? Jesus answered and said unto them, Go and show John again those things which ye do hear and see: the blind receive their sight, and the lame walk, the lepers are cleansed, and the deaf hear, the dead are raised up, and the poor have the gospel preached to them* (Matt. 11:2-5 KJV, emphasis added).

Jesus said, "Tell them about the works." The works will speak for themselves. You don't have to debate or argue with people. Some people will be receptive; others will have a skeptical attitude. But stay bold.

One time I came across several Muslims in Central Park. A couple of them immediately got saved, but a few wanted to discuss and debate. I finally said, "What do you need from God?" One fellow mentioned what he needed, so I laid my hands on him and prayed with boldness and fire. The men were astonished at the words I was using. Why? They marveled at the authority. And they got saved!

Be bold everywhere, just as they were in the Book of Acts. Find somebody. Just walk up to people. They want someone to talk to them and show them the way. People want to come out of their wheelchairs and throw down their canes. Tell people that

God wants to give them a miracle. Try it! Actually...don't try it; do it! Everywhere you go, pray for people—on the streets, in stores and restaurants, on the elevator, waiting in traffic. Many people will be astonished and will believe because of your works.

WILL WE EVER SEE "GREATER WORKS"?

I have prayed over many dead bodies that God would raise them up as a testimony. It hasn't happened yet, but one day it will. It is difficult to raise the dead, especially if that person was saved. It is very hard to call a spirit back that has been to heaven. Do you think they want to come back here? That is the last thing they want to do. So find unsaved people. Give God an opportunity.

Once, at a basketball game as I was moved with compassion looking at a person in a wheelchair, I said, "Lord, when are we going to see the days? I hear about all these miracles. I read about Charles Finney and Smith Wigglesworth. I have studied this all my life. When are we going to see the days where people just come out of their wheelchairs and pop up like popcorn?" He said to me, "When are you going to give Me the opportunity?" God wants to perform the works, but needs willing vessels, you and me, to accomplish them.

Chapter Seventeen

FORSAKING ALL AND ON FIRE FOR GOD

*There went great multitudes with Him: and He turned, and said unto them, If any man come to Me, and hate not his father, and mother, and wife, and children, and brethren, and sisters, yea, and his own life also, he cannot be My disciple. And whosoever doth not bear his cross, and come after Me, cannot be My disciple. For which of you, intending to build a tower, sitteth not down first, and counteth the cost, whether he have sufficient to finish it? Lest haply, after he hath laid the foundation, and is not able to finish it, all that behold it begin to mock him, saying, This man began to build, and was not able to finish. Or what king, going to make war against another king, sitteth not down first, and consulteth whether he be able with ten thousand to meet him that cometh against him with twenty thousand? Or else, while the other is yet a great way off, he sendeth an ambassage, and desireth conditions of peace. **So likewise, whosoever he be of you that forsaketh not all that he hath, he cannot be My disciple.** Salt is good: but if the salt have lost his savour, wherewith shall it be seasoned? It is neither fit for the land, nor yet for the dunghill; but men cast it out. He that hath ears to hear, let him hear* (Luke 14:25-35 KJV, emphasis added).

Did Jesus really mean what He said when He lived on the earth? Did He really say these drastic words? Does God really need to take first priority in your life...before everything else...even your own life? If God was standing right in front of you and said, "Unless you forsake and leave everything, you can't follow Me," and then began walking away, would you follow Him? The disciples did. They left everything and followed Him.

WILL YOU DECIDE TO DIE?

Somewhere along your Christian walk, you will have to make a decision. You need to decide if you're willing to die. I am not talking about death in the physical sense. I am talking about death to the flesh and the things of the world—death to self. Being able to do this doesn't suddenly happen when we meet Jesus. It requires time and sacrifice.

> And there were certain Greeks among them that came up to worship at the feast: the same came therefore to Philip, which was of Bethsaida of Galilee, and desired him, saying, Sir, we would see Jesus. Philip cometh and telleth Andrew: and again Andrew and Philip tell Jesus. And Jesus answered them, saying, The hour is come, that the Son of man should be glorified. Verily, verily, I say unto you, Except a corn of wheat fall into the ground and die, it abideth alone: but if it die, it bringeth forth much fruit (John 12:20-24 KJV).

The disciples who followed Jesus spent three years walking with Him and learning His ways. During their three-year learning experience, Jesus taught them exactly what was required and expected of them. During that time, something was deposited in them that set their hearts burning for the rest of their lives. Something was placed inside them that caused them to die to self and live for Christ. They learned to know Him and were willing to die for Him. But they wouldn't have been able to die for Him if they hadn't known Him first. Somewhere on your walk with God, you must decide if you really want to know and follow Him.

DEATH PRODUCES LIFE

The Message Bible states, "Listen carefully: Unless a grain of wheat is buried in the ground, dead to the world, it is never any more than a grain of wheat. But if it is buried, it sprouts and reproduces itself many times over. In the same way, anyone who holds on to life just as it is destroys life. But if you let it go, reckless in your love, you'll have it forever, real and eternal" (Jn. 12:24-25, The Message Bible). A seed will never produce what it is promised to be, unless it is first buried in the ground and dies.

There is greatness on the inside of every single individual reading this book. God has a promise and a specific plan for your life. A simple seed has the ability to become a productive plant because of what God has placed inside that seed. Each and every person in the same way has the ability to become productive for God, because there is something much bigger than yourself that resides on the inside of you. But the seed can never fulfill its purpose and remains good for nothing if it is not first buried in the ground.

You may have had words spoken over you your whole life. Maybe people have prophesied over you and told you what you were capable of, but unless you have been willing to die to your self, those words will never come to life. We must die. We must die to every kind of selfishness, pride, and false motives. You will recognize those who have died to self. It is clearly evident, not because they tell you they are dead to self, but because they display it. You can see it. There is an hour at hand when God will receive glory in this earth. He will be glorified through those Christians who are followers of Him, who die to themselves. From that death springs forth life.

When we die to self, God comes and resurrects us. First the cross, and then the crown. "He that loveth His life shall lose it: and he that hateth his life in this world shall keep it until life eternal. If any man serve Me, let him follow Me; and where I am there shall also My servant be: if any man serve Me, him will My Father honor" (Jn. 12:25-26 KJV).

WILL YOU DECIDE TO GIVE ALL?

Do you recall the story of the rich young man who asked what he had to do to receive eternal life? Jesus informed him that he must follow the commandments. Having already done this, the man still wondered what he was lacking. Jesus answered him in Matthew 19:21, "If thou wilt be perfect, go and sell that thou hast, and give to the poor, and thou shalt have treasure in heaven: and come and follow Me" (KJV). What a stumbling block for this man! He allowed his wealth to determine his destiny. Then he became very sorrowful because he decided he could not let go of his temporary possessions. Those worthless things had a greater hold of him than God. That rich young man wouldn't give up anything yet had the ability to obtain everything had he followed the King who owns it all.

Once we are saved, we have a decision to make. Are we willing to give up everything? If not, we may be worthless to God. I don't know about you, but I don't want to be in that category, especially when there is already the ability for greatness on the inside of me. The Bible says the salt that lost its saltiness wasn't even good enough for the manure heap (see Luke 14 at the beginning of this chapter).

> *Ye are the salt of the earth: but if the salt have lost his savour, wherewith shall it be salted? It is thenceforth good for nothing, but to be cast out, and to be trodden under foot of men* (Matt. 5:13 KJV).

The Message Bible says, "Let me tell you why you are here. You're here to be salt-seasoning that brings out the God-flavors of the earth. If you lose your saltiness, how will people taste godliness? You've lost your usefulness and will end up in the garbage."

In this Scripture, God chooses to use salt to describe us. Interestingly, salt can lose its savor, but salt can never lose its potency. When it ceases to heal, it starts to corrupt. That is why Jesus said that a lukewarm church is worse than a cold one, because men cast it out. Christianity is more than just about you.

Others are watching how we portray Jesus, and how we live our lives can determine the eternal destiny of others. Jesus used very strong words here because He loves others and wants them to know Him as well.

ARE YOUR WORKS HOT, OR COLD, OR NEITHER?

And unto the angel of the church of Laodiceans write; These things saith the Amen, the faithful and true witness, the beginning of the creation of God; I know thy works, that thou art neither cold nor hot: I would thou weren't cold or hot. So then because thou art lukewarm, and neither cold nor hot, I will spew thee out of my mouth (Rev. 3:14-16 KJV).

If I were to measure your temperature with a spiritual thermometer, what would it read? Some of you might say, "Well, I go to church and I always show up on time," and expect your thermometer to read 100 degrees Fahrenheit—on fire for God. If the only sacrifice that we as Christians can make, is getting to church on Sunday, and we expect to get a reward, something is wrong. Unfortunately, in many cases, that is the extent of our Christian duty. There are those who boast over not missing a service, or those who brag about being a member, or teaching a class for a certain number of years.

However, Jesus was blunt. He meant what He said when He declared, "Anyone who does not take his cross and follow Me is not worthy of Me" (Mt. 10:38). Is Jesus kind, loving, and merciful? Yes, He is, but He cannot tolerate lukewarm Christianity. He went to a cross and died. There is no greater love than this—that a man would lay down his life for another. Have you picked up your cross and carried what He has required of you?

LUKEWARM CHRISTIANITY

In Revelation chapter 3, the church at Laodicea was being evaluated for its works. "I know thy works, that thou art neither cold nor hot." Jesus confronted this church boldly, saying that the church was basically "sitting in the middle." Jesus then said these words, "So then because you are lukewarm and neither cold nor hot, I will spit you out of My mouth."

This is an unbelievably strong statement: "I will spit you out." Jesus did not say, "I will brush you aside," but "I will spit you out." There is no room for compromise when we read this statement. Lukewarm is unacceptable to God; He cannot stand the taste of it. And if Jesus, the head of the church, feels this way, then surely His church, His followers, should feel the same way.

Let's use iced tea as an analogy. Iced tea is pretty good, especially when you live in the South. And in the North, they make a great cup of hot tea. Hot or cold is fine, but who likes warm tea? Yeech! No one. It is distasteful. Lukewarm Christianity doesn't cut it either. The most amazing statement implied here is that God would rather you not serve Him at all if you can't serve Him wholeheartedly. Serving Him wholeheartedly is serving Him with everything you have. It goes back to believing with our heart, confessing it with our mouth, and living out our faith.

If you are a true servant on fire with the love and passion of a real Christian, you will not be able to accept mediocrity in your Christian life. When you are in tune with the Holy Ghost, you will smell religion a mile away; you will detest the very essence of mediocre Christianity; and you will run miles away from it.

When Jesus walked the earth, there was one thing that He couldn't tolerate—religion. He couldn't stomach it. It had no place in Him. He didn't have a problem with the world. Sinners loved Jesus. It was the religious people He had to contend with. Religious people honor God with their lips but their hearts are far from Him. Just as there were in Jesus' day, so are there present-day Pharisees who go to church and get into the worship mode, but their hearts are truly far from Him.

AMERICA—A LUKEWARM NATION

At the present time, the American church seems to have an appetite for lukewarm Christianity. America is like the church of Laodicea, the most affluent region of Bible times. Resources abounded and they seemingly had everything they could ask for, yet their material success was their greatest demise. Their dependence on God was exchanged for reliance on riches. The result was a lukewarm people.

Whereas, in Africa, I have seen desperate people longing for a touch from God. They travel and arrive 14 days in advance to attend a crusade. They lay outside, sleeping in the mud and waiting in expectation. Their hearts are ravenous for the things of God. Six days before a crusade, 20,000-30,000 people are in place. And what are we concerned about? Having the right temperature set in the sanctuary along with saving our favorite cushioned seats.

They are not distracted by so many of the material things that pull our attention away from God. They don't have the conveniences and comforts that we are accustomed to. God is their only hope. *Desperate* seems almost an inadequate word for what they display. If they are dirty, they don't have indoor plumbing at their disposal. If someone has a medical emergency, there is no ambulance to call or hospital to rush to. When they are hungry, they don't have access to a refrigerator in the next room or a grocery store down the street. God is their only plan.

The African nation of Nigeria, which includes millions and millions of people, is currently experiencing one of the greatest moves of God in all of Africa. Brother Reinhard Bonnke, a well-known evangelist to Africa has been preaching in various crusades throughout the region. At one crusade 1.2 million people arrived and 700,000 were saved. Along with salvations, people are being raised from the dead. Can you believe it? A pastor who was dead and reeking of embalming fluid for three weeks was placed in a church, and while a service was in progress, he literally jumped out of his coffin. Those churches are raising the dead, whereas the modern-day church in America is "dead."

Lukewarmness has wounded the church more than anything else, and it is hurting the world, causing many people to go to hell. As Americans, we insist on the easy and the comfortable.

We work very hard making sure everything suits us just right. We walk into the church and make sure the temperature in the building meets everybody's needs. The seats must be comfortable and the service, not too long. We don't want anyone to get hungry or miss their Sunday brunch. Can you believe this? Do you understand that our actions are a slap in the face of Jesus? We are as pathetic as the people who spat on Him and pierced Him.

All too often people who come off the streets and into the church never stay for very long. Why? They know there is more to life than they see in the church. We have been hard on the sinner and have preached judgment and punishment. Whereas, to the saved, we continue to preach grace, grace, God's grace—it's okay to sin because He forgives. We've had the message backwards. We should be preaching grace to the sinner. We need to preach Jesus first. They need the very One who has come to help them clean up their mess. They need Jesus. They also need to see a church that is desperate for the things of God, a church that will press in no matter the cost. But unfortunately, the world does not want what most churches have. They spit out the lukewarmness as well, and keep searching for a life of meaning.

CHECK YOUR SPIRITUAL TEMPERATURE

What is your spiritual temperature? Are you simply going through the motions of your Christianity? Do you come to church on Sunday and then live like the world the rest of the week? If Jesus were to take your temperature and it revealed a lukewarm reading, how would you respond? Do you think He would put up with that in your life? He has done so much for us, more than we can even comprehend. Jesus Christ suffered and died; He endured indescribable anguish for you. He bore beatings, floggings, mockery, and crucifixion for you. When they spit on Him and pierced His side, it was for you. When they whipped Him, He did that for you too. If you were the only one on the face of this earth who needed salvation, He would have laid down His life just for you. Have we done all we can do to show Him our love in return?

Are you really one of His followers, one of His disciples? Does being a Christian simply mean that God does something for you? Are you doing anything for Him? All over the earth people are standing up in our pulpits and saying, "This is what God wants to do for you." The message of Christianity has been watered down, and consequently, we have "drips" as Christians. We must take note of people like the Nigerians and heed the example of those who live in desperation for God.

Are you hot? Are you cold? Are you lukewarm? God is so gracious and compassionate that there is no reason for us not to be on fire. As you forsake all else, He will set you ablaze. There is more on the inside of you. There is greatness! You are here on this earth for a divine reason, and God wants you to fulfill the purpose for your life. Wherever you work, God has placed you in that job to be a messenger for that workplace. If you go to school, God has placed you there to be a messenger with this light. Christians need to live like Christians and say, "I will go where You want me to go. I will say what You want me to say. I will do what You want me to do. Thy will be done."

Chapter Eighteen

PETER, PAUL, AND STEPHEN— MEN WHO GAVE ALL

SIMON PETER

Peter was a fisherman who owned a fishing business. It was a common job for a common man. He had heard this wild guy named John the Baptist, the "talk of the town," shouting out in the wilderness, "There is One that cometh after me whose shoes I am not worthy to bear." John was always talking about One who was coming...One who was coming. Then to Peter's surprise, one day he turned around and heard a voice, "Come follow Me and I will make you fishers of men." None other than Jesus stood before him. Imagine what it would have been like to be Peter at that moment. Without hesitation Peter followed.

Who Is This Jesus?

Imagine you yourself, getting up, leaving everything you are familiar and comfortable with and following the one they call Jesus. You journey with Him and experience life as He lives it. You are there when the very first miracle takes place at the wedding of Cana of Galilee. You are there with Him as multitudes touch Him and many are made whole. You are there with Him when blind Bartimaeus shouts out. You see Him at the Mount of Transfiguration. His clothes become white. You see the glory of the Lord and you hear the audible voice of God say, "This is My beloved Son, listen to Him."

At another time, Peter saw Jesus walking on the water and said, "Lord, if it is you, bid me to come!" And Peter started to step out on the water. Imagine with me again as if you were Peter. While sitting on the edge of the boat, you turn to lift one leg out, in nervous anticipation. You know that it is Christ who stands before you. You carefully lift the other leg and hesitantly touch the water with one toe. Slowly, you come to your feet and in the next moment you start walking. You are walking on water! You are not walking on ice or standing on a raft. You are walking on water.

You are there when the woman with the issue of blood gets healed. You are there when Jesus multiplies the bread and the fish. You see Jairus' daughter rise up from the dead. You are there when Jesus says, "Lazarus, come forth!" You are Jesus' right-hand companion for three years. You walk and talk with Him, eat and spend time with Him, and intimately get to know Him and His purpose in life.

Then one day, Jesus point-blank asks you a question, "Who do people say that I am?" "Some say John the Baptist; others say Elijah or Jeremiah or one of the prophets," is your response. Then Christ says, "Who do *you* say I am?"

*Who do **you** say I am?...*

Without hesitation, Peter stood up and said, "You are the Christ, the Son of the living God." Jesus responded, "Blessed are you, Simon son of Jonah, for this was not revealed to you by man, but by My Father in heaven. Upon this rock (Peter) I will build My church, and the gates of hell will not overcome it" (see Mt. 16:13-18).

What Do You Mean "Not Converted"?

Jesus was going to build His church upon Peter. What a great promise! The beginning of the New Testament church would start with Peter.

Then sometime later, during the Last Supper, Jesus said to Peter,

Simon, Simon, satan has asked to sift you as wheat. But I have prayed for you, Simon, that your faith may not fail. And when you have turned back, strengthen your brothers (Luke 22:31-32).

Jesus was praying for Peter, and something radical was about to happen. Jesus' instructions to Peter were, "When you have turned back, strengthen your brothers." The King James Version says, "When you are converted...." What went through Peter's head when Jesus said, "When you are converted"? I am sure Peter was aghast. "What do you mean 'turn back'? What do you mean 'converted'?" He might have been thinking, *Pray for me? I won't ever turn away, so I won't need to turn back to You. You might want to be praying for Judas—but praying for me? How about praying for Thomas? I'm Your right-hand man. I'm with You. What do You mean "pray for me"? What do You mean "turn back"? I left my fishing business for You. I am converted. What more do You want?*

*Then Peter said, "Lord, **I am ready** to go with You to prison and to death"* (Lk. 22:33, emphasis added).

Peter said, "I am ready to go anywhere with You! I am ready to die for You. I am ready to be thrown in jail. I am ready. I give You my life. Do whatever You want with it." Jesus responded, "I tell you, Peter, before the rooster crows today, you will deny three times that you know Me" (Lk. 22:34).

Ready or Not

"Lord, I am ready to go anywhere for You. I am Your servant. I will go where You want me to go. I will do what You want me to do. I will say what You want me to say. I will be whatever You want me to be. Take my life. I will die for You," Peter declared. Yet Jesus responded, "You will deny three times that you know Me."

Just as Peter thought he was ready to live and die for Christ, so do many people think likewise today. If you ask many

Christians in America if they are ready for revival, if they are ready to die for Christ, they will most likely respond, "I am ready. I will do anything for Him." But are we really ready? While some can't even find time to attend a mid-week church service or a Bible study group, they still insist they are ready to die for Him. Others wouldn't think of missing their favorite TV show for a church prayer meeting or give up a football game for an outreach, but yet they declare they would give their life for Him.

People believe that because they have professed to be Christians their entire life and have attended church for many years, they are ready. But consider Peter who himself spent three years with Jesus—eating, sleeping, talking, traveling. He saw great miracles and felt the power of God flow through his hands. Yet he still needed a heartfelt conversion. Many people are seeing and doing good things—going to church, reading the Bible, praying—but they still have not been converted. They have not *turned back* to Christ.

Even though Peter wasn't as ready as he thought he was, Jesus had prophesied that upon Peter the church would be built. The anointing would come on Peter; but how would it begin? What would happen in the process?

Following at a Distance

*Then seizing Him, they led Him away and took Him into the house of the high priest. Peter **followed at a distance**. But when they had kindled a fire in the middle of the courtyard and had sat down together, Peter sat down with them. A servant girl saw him seated there in the firelight. She looked closely at him and said, "This man was with Him." But he denied it. "Woman, I don't know Him," he said. A little later someone else saw him and said, "You also are one of them." "Man, I am not!" Peter replied. About an hour later another asserted, "Certainly this fellow was with Him, for he is a Galilean." Peter replied, "Man, I don't know what* *you're talking about!" Just as he was speaking, the rooster crowed* (Luke 22:54-60, emphasis added).

After Jesus had been arrested, Peter followed *at a distance.*

What makes someone a follower? Is it someone who physically goes through the motions of coming along after someone? Peter went through the motions of following, but along the way, he denied the one he was supposedly following.

Peter said he was willing to go to prison and to die for Christ, but Jesus knew differently. He knew that Peter still needed to have a genuine conversion experience. As Peter "followed" at a distance, three different people questioned his association with Jesus, and each time, Peter denied knowing Him.

The Lord turned and looked straight at Peter. Then Peter remembered the word the Lord had spoken to him: "Before the rooster crows today, you will disown Me three times." And he went outside and wept bitterly (Luke 22:61-62).

Had Peter been following Christ or just going through the motions? I believe that when he stepped out to follow Jesus, he was saved; but was he a true disciple?

What is a true disciple? A disciple looks like Jesus and a disciple acts like Jesus, doing the very same things He did. True followers of Christ make a difference in other people's lives. The greatest character trait of a Christian is love, and the greatest proof of love is giving. Jesus said to love the Lord with all your heart, soul, mind, and strength and to love your neighbor as yourself. Who is your neighbor? Read the "Good Samaritan" story. A neighbor is anybody who needs you. True followers are willing to lay down their lives for someone else.

Peter's life at this point presents a prophetic picture of the church in America going through the motions of following Christ, but not making a difference in anybody's life along the way. There are supposedly millions of Christians in America, a church on every corner, but where are the followers? Christianity is not just something we are; it is something we do.

A Life-Changing Conversion

Peter's life was about to change. Notice that right after the third denial, Jesus, His Master, turned and looked upon Peter. As He looked straight into Peter's eyes, Peter realized he wasn't where he was supposed to be, and suddenly there was an encounter. He wept uncontrollably, unreservedly, and bitterly. He cried out and cried out. Peter had *a conversion.*

Brothers and sisters in Christ, the church needs to have a conversion—a conversion where there is no backsliding and no denying, a conversion where no one needs to be told to win the lost because they will already be doing so. Peter was suddenly awakened. He saw things completely different. He saw through the eyeglasses of eternity, and saw what life was about. He saw his Lord and experienced a life-changing realization that he wasn't where he needed to be. He had an encounter.

I have seen people all over the country have that same encounter, and when they experience it, they are changed. Their passion becomes God—morning, noon, and night.

When Jesus told Peter he would deny Him three times, He may have sounded unnecessarily strong, harsh, or negative; but His words were the truth. He wanted Peter to accomplish all that Peter was called to do. A process had to happen. The church must also go through a process to experience a conversion.

Do you know what provokes a revival? Those piercing messages that convict us and reveal where we really are in our walk with God. Revivals have started with messages that our normal churches could not handle. They couldn't handle John Wesley. They kicked him out of every mainline church because his message was too strong. Many people couldn't tolerate Charles Finney or George Whitefield. Others disliked what Jonathan Edwards had to say. The words of these men revealed the painful truth, and embarrassed and hurt the listeners. Too often, most people would rather hear the feel-good messages telling us how we can be free, how we can be blessed, how we can be healed, and what God will do to make our lives better. But to experience a genuine conversion, we must be told the truth and realize that we are not where we are supposed to be.

A Different Peter

You never see the same Peter after this conversion experience. God absolutely wrecked him. I believe if you would have seen a picture of Peter at the moment he was converted, you would have seen a total mess. He knew he had denied his Lord and he had never felt worse in his life. Yet it had been prophesied that he would start the church. It was his destiny to do great things. The Lord prayed for him and he received a conversion.

Now let's fast-forward to the church of Acts where Peter is standing firm and tall. Suddenly, the once ashamed Peter who had denied his Lord, who had practiced that in-the-closet Christianity, steps out so that everybody can see. Peter now preaches with boldness.

> *But Peter, standing up with the eleven, lifted up his voice, and said unto them, Ye men of Judea, and all ye that dwell at Jerusalem, be this known unto you, and hearken to my words: for these are not drunken, as ye suppose, seeing it is but the third hour of the day. But this is that which was spoken by the prophet Joel; and it shall come to pass in the last days, saith God, I will pour out My spirit upon all flesh: and your sons and your daughters shall prophesy, and your young men shall see visions, and your old men shall dream dreams* (Acts 2:14-17 KJV).

In Acts 3, we see Peter about to enter a gate called Beautiful. He is not denying his Lord these days. His eyes are open. He looks at people differently. In the past, he would have walked right past a disabled person, but not now. He is wearing the eyeglasses of eternity.

> *Now Peter and John went up together into the temple at the hour of prayer, being the ninth hour. And a certain man lame from his mother's womb was carried, whom they laid daily*

*at the gate of the temple which is called Beautiful, to ask
alms of them that entered into the temple; Who seeing Peter
and John about to go into the temple asked an alms. And
Peter, fastening his eyes upon him with John, said, Look on
us. And he gave heed unto them, expecting to receive something of them. Then Peter said, Silver and gold have I none;
but such as I have give I thee: In the name of Jesus Christ of
Nazareth rise up and walk* (Acts 3:1-7 KJV).

Now when he sees hurting people, Peter stops. "I don't have
any silver and gold, but I'll give you what I do have. In the name
of Jesus Christ, walk." Peter grabs the man by the hand and pulls
him up. Instantly, the man's feet and ankles become strong. Peter
is not the same and neither is this man.

Peter continues to be strong in the Lord and is used in
miraculous ways. Some people will die in his presence because of
their dishonesty, and other people will throw bodies in his
shadow for healing.

God is not a respecter of persons and will use anyone on
this earth. In fact, He wants to use you. Give God your vessel. Give Him your voice, your hands and feet. Stop following
at a distance. Draw closer. Look into His eyes and turn back
to Him.

SAUL, WHO WAS ALSO CALLED PAUL

One of the worst enemies of the church in his day, Saul was
merciless in his pursuit of any Christian. Stopping at each and
every house, he drug off Christian men and women and had
them thrown into prison simply because they confessed that
Jesus was the Savior and Lord of their lives.

At one particular time, after listening to the riveting testimony of Stephen and his speech accusing the Sanhedrin of
resisting the Holy Spirit and betraying Jesus Christ, Paul
unmovingly consented to Stephen's gruesome death by stoning.
And Saul did not stop there.

Saul Changes Direction

> *And Saul, yet breathing out threatenings and slaughter against the disciples of the Lord, went unto the high priest, and desired of him letters to Damascus to the synagogues, that if he found any of this way, whether they were men or women, he might bring them bound unto Jerusalem. And as he journeyed, he came near Damascus: and suddenly there shined round about him a light from heaven* (Acts 9:1-3 KJV).

Saul had been traveling in one direction...the wrong direction. How many of you know that if a certain someone ever got saved, you would declare for sure that there is a God? I remember a particular bully in elementary school. He was one of those bullies who would think nothing of charging at you and throwing a punch...for no reason. All through middle school and high school, I always thought that if that guy would ever get saved, number one: it would be a miracle; number two, there was a God; and number three, there is no doubt this Christianity thing is real. Just recently, I found out this guy was radically saved and he is attending Bible school. Praise the Lord!

Saul was of the same breed. He was the worst of the worst. Fortunately, the Bible says that suddenly a light shone down from heaven and knocked him "off his horse." And when he got up from the ground, he could no longer see.

Saul was a chosen vessel before he was saved. Did you know that there are chosen vessels all across the land? There are calls on people's lives, regardless of what they are doing or how they are living now. Saul was a chosen vessel to bring the gospel.

Shortly after this experience, Saul became a follower of Christ. After meeting with Ananias, Saul regained his sight and soon began to preach.

From the Hunter to the Hunted

> *And immediately there fell from his eyes as it had been scales: and he received sight forthwith, and arose, and was*

baptized. And when he had received meat, he was strength-
ened. Then was Saul certain days with the disciples which
were at Damascus. And straightway he preached Christ in
the synagogues, that he is the Son of God. But all that
heard him were amazed, and said; Is not this he that
destroyed them which called on this name in Jerusalem, and
came hither for that intent, that he might bring them bound
unto the chief priests? But Saul increased the more in
strength, and confounded the Jews which dwelt at Damas-
cus, proving that this is very Christ. And after that many
days were fulfilled, the Jews took counsel to kill him: but
their laying wait was known of Saul. And they watched the
gates day and night to kill him (Acts 9:18-24 KJV).

In this very same chapter of Acts, we find Saul (who had
once taken a stand in complete defiance of those who followed
Jesus Christ and who was once the persecutor) is now the persecuted—a follower himself. Verse 24 says that the Jews were waiting day and night to kill the man.

Paul's experience wasn't a "slow" conversion. I believe what
happened is indicative of people who get touched by God. I
believe that when you meet Jesus, it is an instant experience.

Paul became radical for God instantly, and immediately he
began to cause havoc. One day he was sentencing Christian Jews
to death for their faith in Jesus Christ; not many days later the
Jews he had previously associated with were trying to kill him
for the very same reason. But God had a plan for this chosen vessel. The Jews would not kill him, and he would eventually write
two thirds of the New Testament.

Our Message Needs to Be Extreme

During Paul's life and in many other stories in the Scriptures, people either loved Jesus or they hated Him. They would
die for Him or want to kill Him. There was no middle ground. It
is still the same today. You find people for Him or against Him.
No one ever said, "Well that Jesus, He is all right. I was there
that time He healed someone and their arm grew out. He's not a

bad guy. I was there and ate some bread and fish that time He fed the multitudes, and I was there when He turned water into wine—that was pretty cool. I like the meetings; they are not so bad. I have some problems with things like people ripping down a roof to get to Jesus. One time I saw Jesus spit on His hands and put it on someone's face to heal him—that wasn't so sanitary. I'm not really sure about His methods, but He really is not that bad." No! You don't find anybody saying things like that. They either loved Him and would die for Him, or they wanted to kill Him. It was *extreme*.

While at the Michigan crusade, many people confronted us about our "hard and negative" messages. Could it be that we just don't like getting our feathers ruffled? We can handle maybe a service or two of preaching that makes us squirm, but not for six months. Many want to run back to the feel-good stuff, the healing and Holy Ghost messages. Yes, God wants us healthy, blessed, whole, and with provision, but God wants us ultimately to fulfill His purpose and to preach the gospel to a lost and dying world. Every revivalist comes with a hard message. Awakenings will come with hard, convicting messages that pierce the heart. Think about the Cross and what Jesus did and then tell me our messages should not convict or condemn. The message seems too hard because we have taken our Christianity too lightly.

People come to our meetings and get totally transformed, or they call claim heresy. You tell me—what looks more like God and what pleases Him: people coming into church for only an hour once a week, or people weeping for lost humanity every day, beseeching God for more power every day, and going out with passion every day? I believe that in these last days, people will do exactly those things. Either you will die for Christ and daily give Him every last bit of your life, or you will want to kill Him.

The Boldness of Paul

In Acts chapter 18, we find Paul in danger again.

And when Silas and Timotheus were come from Macedonia, Paul was pressed in the spirit, and testified to the Jews that

Jesus was Christ. And when they opposed themselves, and blasphemed, he shook his raiment, and said unto them, Your blood be upon your own heads; I am clean: from henceforth I will go unto the Gentiles. And he departed thence, and entered into a certain man's house, named Justus, one that worshipped God, whose house joined hard to the synagogue. And Crispus, the chief ruler of the synagogue, believed on the Lord with all his house; and many of the Corinthians hearing believed, and were baptized. Then spake the Lord to Paul in the night by a vision, Be not afraid, but speak, and hold not thy peace: for I am with thee, and no man shall set on thee to hurt thee: for I have much people in this city. And he continued there a year and six months, teaching the word of God among them (Acts 18:5-11 KJV).

Here Paul came to Corinth and already he was in danger. This man had a conversion, took his faith very seriously, and acted as a true disciple of Christ. He preached boldly that Christ is the Son of God. What we need in America are true Christians like Paul, true followers after the heart of God, who will boldly go and tell the world.

In Acts chapter 19, Paul entered the city of Ephesus where he found some disciples and baptized them in the name of the Lord Jesus. Following this Paul continued to proclaim the name of the Lord Jesus.

And he went into the synagogue, and spake boldly for the space of three months, disputing and persuading the things concerning the kingdom of God. But when divers were hardened, and believed not, but spake evil of that way before the multitude, he departed from them, and separated the disciples, disputing daily in the school of one Tyrannus. And this continued by the space of two years; so that all they which dwelt in Asia heard the word of the Lord Jesus, both Jews and Greeks (Acts 19:8-10 KJV).

At this time, the population of Ephesus was approximately a half million people. To reach that many *people* in two years, the

Christians must have been driven. They must have gone every-where. That was their focus every day.

The purpose of the church is to win souls. It is more than just about workshops, coffee, and fellowship. Jesus said, "Upon this rock I will build My church and the gates of hell shall not prevail against it." We are talking about an offensive church kick-ing down the very gates of hell—a very forward, vocal, and bold church. Is that what the churches in America look like? No. Here in America, it seems like the gates of hades are invading the gates of heaven. Unfortunately, hell has come and is infiltrating many churches, and in some cases, permeating our pulpits.

Paul Causes an Uproar Everywhere, Even in Hell

And God wrought special miracles by the hands of Paul: so that from his body were brought unto the sick handkerchiefs or aprons, and the diseases departed from them, and the evil spirits went out of them. Then certain of the vagabond Jews, exorcists, took upon them to call over them which had evil spirits the name of the Lord Jesus, saying, We adjure you by Jesus whom Paul preacheth. And there were seven sons of one Sceva, a Jew, and chief of the priests, which did so. And the evil spirit answered and said, Jesus I know, and Paul I know; but who are ye? (Acts 19:11-15 KJV).

Let me ask you a question. Does the devil even know that you exist? Does the devil know that you are on this earth? Are you doing anything, as Paul did, to irritate and upset the devil's kingdom? Paul wanted to be known in hell. The evil spirit said, "Jesus I know, and Paul I know, but who are you?" Are the demons wondering, "Who are you?"

Paul upset the devil's kingdom and caused an uproar wher-ever he went. Can you imagine a revival taking place and finding a whole city in confusion? Now some of you may be thinking, *That can't be God. God is not the author of confusion, but maintains order. When God comes, everyone is happy.* Well, my friend, read the Bible. The fact is, when God comes, all hell breaks loose. Do you want hell to break loose? Do you want to stir things up?

Paul Would Not be Moved

> And from Miletus he sent to Ephesus, and called the elders
> of the church. And when they were come to him, he said
> unto them, Ye know, from the first day that I came into
> Asia, after what manner I have been with you at all sea-
> sons, serving the Lord with all humility of mind, and with
> many tears, and temptations, which befell me by the lying
> in wait of the Jews: and how I kept back nothing that was
> profitable unto you, but have shown you, and have
> taught you publicly, and from house to house, testifying
> both to the Jews, and also to the Greeks, repentance
> toward God, and faith toward our Lord Jesus Christ. And
> now, behold, I go bound in the spirit unto Jerusalem, not
> knowing the things that shall befall me there: save that
> the Holy Ghost witnesseth in every city, saying that
> bonds and afflictions abide me. But **none of these things
> move me**, neither count I my life dear unto myself, so that
> I might finish my course with joy, and the ministry, which I
> have received of the Lord Jesus, to testify the gospel of the
> grace of God (Acts 20:17-24 KJV, emphasis added).

Here is true Christianity. "None of these things move me."
True Christians will not be moved by anything but God. Whip
us, beat us, shipwreck us, stone us, or even crucify us. We know
our God, and we will not be shaken.

But wait a minute…here in America, if we are a little finan-
cially strapped one month, we get down and depressed. We actually decide not to go to church, and all of a sudden, we're blaming
God. Or if we're feeling physically ill, we question why God has-
n't healed us and become resentful and angry. Sometimes people
will purposely commit a sin, thinking they are "getting back" at
God. The Bible says that nothing moved the apostle Paul.

We Will Suffer Just as Paul Suffered

Paul expressed his heart and did not neglect his responsibility to declare the will of God. When writing to the Galatians, the
apostle talked about being crucified with Christ. He died daily,

and Christ lived within him. Paul did not boast about himself, but bragged about his sufferings and weaknesses that revealed Christ's strength.

> *Are they ministers of Christ? (I speak as a fool) I am more; in labours more abundant, in stripes above measure, in prisons more frequent, in deaths oft. Of the Jews five times received I forty stripes save one. Thrice was I beaten with rods, once I was stoned, thrice I suffered shipwreck, a night and a day I have been in the deep; in journeyings often, in perils of waters, in perils of robbers, in perils by mine own countrymen, in perils by the heathen, in perils in the city, in perils in the wilderness, in perils in the sea, in perils among false brethren; in weariness and painfulness, in watchings often, in hunger and thirst, in fastings often, in cold and nakedness. Beside those things that are without, that which cometh upon me daily, the care of all the churches (2 Cor. 11:23-28 KJV).*

Paul encountered many trials and tribulations, yet he continued to live righteously. The Bible says that all who live godly will suffer much persecution. America is not exempt from this declaration. How much persecution have you suffered? I challenge you to live godly in Christ. If the amount of persecution determined your guilt as a Christian, would there be enough evidence to convict you?

> *But thou hast fully known my doctrine, manner of life, purpose, faith, longsuffering, charity, patience, persecutions, afflictions which came unto me at Antioch, at Iconium, at Lystra; what persecutions I endured: but out of them all the Lord delivered me. Yea, and all that will live godly in Christ Jesus shall suffer persecution. But evil men and seducers shall wax worse and worse, deceiving, and being deceived. But continue thou in the things which thou hast learned them; and that from a child thou hast known the holy scriptures, which are able to make thee wise unto salvation through faith which is in Christ Jesus (2 Tim. 3:10-15 KJV).*

Paul Kept the Faith

At the end of his second letter to Timothy, Paul mentioned his satisfaction with the life he had lived for Christ and his longing to see his Lord.

> *I charge thee therefore before God, and the Lord Jesus Christ, who shall judge the quick and the dead at His appearing and His kingdom; preach the word; be instant in season, out of season; reprove, rebuke, exhort with all longsuffering and doctrine....But watch thou in all things, endure afflictions, do the work of an evangelist, make full proof of thy ministry. For I am now ready to be offered, and the time of my departure is at hand. **I have fought a good fight, I have finished my course, I have kept the faith: henceforth there is laid up for me a crown of righteousness, which the Lord, the righteous judge, shall give me at that day: and not to me only, but unto all them also that love His appearing** (2 Tim. 4:1-2,5-8 KJV, emphasis added).*

Nothing moved Paul. Nothing moved him because he knew that there was a victor's crown laid up for him and Jesus was watching. He had run a race. He hadn't looked behind. He had pressed on. May we press on with boldness as well, unmovable in our faith, causing an uproar wherever we go.

STEPHEN

> *And in those days, when the number of the disciples was multiplied, there arose a murmuring of the Grecians against the Hebrews, because their widows were neglected in the daily ministration. Then the twelve called the multitude of the disciples unto them, and said, It is not reason that we should leave the word of God, and serve tables. Wherefore, brethren, look ye out among you seven men of honest report, full of the Holy Ghost and wisdom, whom we may appoint over this business. But we will give ourselves continually to prayer, and to the ministry of the word. And the saying pleased the whole multitude: **and they chose Stephen, a man full of faith and of the Holy Ghost, and***

Philip, and Prochorus, and Nicanor, and Timon, and Par-
menas, and Nicolas a proselyte of Antioch: whom they set
before the apostles: and when they had prayed, they laid
their hands on them. And the word of God increased; and
the number of the disciples multiplied in Jerusalem greatly;
and a great company of the priests were obedient to the
faith. **And Stephen, full of faith and power, did great**
wonders and miracles among the people. *Then there arose*
certain of the synagogue, which is called the synagogue of
the Libertines, and Cyrenians, and Alexandrians, and of
them of Cilicia and of Asia, disputing with Stephen. And
they were not able to resist the wisdom of the spirit by
which he spake (Acts 6:1-5,9-10 KJV, emphasis added).

The ministry in the church had grown to such an extent that the disciples decided it was essential to choose some people to help them. They couldn't just choose anyone however. They needed people full of the Holy Ghost—people who had a heart for God.

Gifts, talents, and abilities are nice, but a heart for God is essential. Every single person in ministry should be full of the Holy Ghost, full of fire, and full of faith; and they should desire to do signs and wonders. They found one such man in Stephen.

A Shining Life

In the short Scripture passage above, we can determine several important things about Stephen.

In the beginning stages of his ministry, Stephen was already full of faith and the Holy Ghost, and was known for his willingness to serve others. And because of his faith and the indwelling Holy Spirit, Stephen possessed a power that enabled him to do great works and miracles for the Lord. Not everyone was happy about these wonders though.

Needless to say, this did not deter him. Instead of spending time in the comfort of the synagogue, he went out among the unsaved world. He was a light shining in the middle of the darkness. Although some members of the synagogue attempted to argue with Stephen and discredit him, they were no match for his God-given wisdom.

> *Then they suborned men, which said, We have heard him speak blasphemous words against Moses, and against God. And they stirred up the people, and the elders, and the scribes, and came upon him, and caught him, and brought him to the council, and set up false witnesses, which said, This man ceaseth not to speak blasphemous words against this holy place, and the law: for we have heard him say, that this Jesus of Nazareth shall destroy this place, and shall change the customs which Moses delivered us. And all that sat in the council, looking stedfastly on him, saw his face as it had been the face of an angel* (Acts 6:11-15 KJV).

Stephen was radical in his faith and turned the place upside down. Suddenly without warning, he was thrown into jail. Guilty of loving God and hungering for righteousness, he was instead falsely accused of blaspheming against God and was tried before the council.

Standing and Dying for the Truth

Without apology or taming his words, Stephen spoke the truth and stood for his faith to the very end. After Stephen spoke before the Sanhedrin and condemned them for resisting the Holy Spirit and murdering Jesus, the high priest and his fellow councilmen became furious.

> *When they heard these things, they were cut to the heart, and they gnashed on him with their teeth* (Acts 7:54 KJV).

The religious Sanhedrin thought they knew everything there was to know about God; but God came in a way they didn't understand. They were waiting for the Messiah, but when He came, they didn't recognize Him. What did they do? They killed Him. They had waited for generations and generations for the Messiah, and the very One whom they had been praying for, they killed. And they were determined to kill His followers too.

But he, being full of the Holy Ghost, looked up steadfastly into heaven, and saw the glory of God, and Jesus standing on the right hand of God, and said, Behold, I see the heavens opened, and the Son of man standing on the right hand of God. Then they cried out with a loud voice, and stopped their ears, and ran upon him with one accord. And cast him out of the city, and stoned him: and the witnesses laid down their clothes at a young man's feet, whose name was **Saul**. *And they stoned Stephen, calling upon God, and saying Lord Jesus, receive my spirit. And he kneeled down, and cried with a loud voice, Lord, lay not this sin to their charge. And when he had said this, he fell asleep* (Acts 7:55-60 KJV, emphasis added).

Can you imagine being stoned? Rocks forcefully thrown at you in anger. Vile words screamed in your face. Flesh being torn from your body and blood flowing from head to toe. And all the while that Stephen is suffering indescribable anguish, a certain young man named Saul looks on.

True Christianity Breeds Other True Christians

Although Saul consented to Stephen's death, he must have been affected by Stephen's determination and tenacity. I believe he heard the words that Stephen uttered at the end, "Father, forgive them." He must have been there when Stephen was arrested and when Stephen stood boldly for his faith. Stephen was hardcore. He hadn't minced words when he stood before the council defending the faith and said, "Ye stiffnecked and uncircumcised in heart and ears, ye do always resist the Holy Ghost: as your fathers did, so do ye" (Acts 7:51 KJV). The man was intense. Stephen was definitely not seeker-friendly. He was Holy-Spirit inspired. I believe Saul watched this whole encounter and was affected by it.

When you are on fire, you will set others ablaze. They asked John Wesley what was the key to the first Great Awakening and he stated, "I set myself on fire and others come watch me burn. And when they see me burn they reach out to touch because they want to burn too." As Saul watched Stephen, he saw what a real Christian looked like. He saw someone totally committed, even to death. He was touched by the boldness of Stephen, and it changed his life forever. When Saul finally got saved, he became just as radical for his Lord as Stephen had been during his life.

As with many others, I will never forget what happened on September 11th, when terrorists attacked New York City and the Pentagon. My brother had been in one of the World Trade Center towers and was able to escape. Did you know that it was only 19 individuals who committed this horrific act? Only 19. As sick and demented and deceived as they were, you cannot escape the fact that they were willing to die for what they believed. As pathetic and twisted as their beliefs were, they were still willing to die for them. Where is that same unswerving dedication, passion, and commitment in the church? How many people do you actually know who would die for the sake of the gospel? Are we constantly thinking—morning, noon, and night—how we are going to destroy the works of the enemy? Are we always planning how to share the gospel—morning, noon, and night? That commitment and willingness to surrender all will attract others to the truth. They will want something that is worth dying for. True followers of Jesus will breed other true followers of Jesus.

Chapter Nineteen

SOLDIERS IN THE ARMY
OF THE LORD

Assemble ourselves, and come, all ye heathen, and gather yourselves together round about: thither cause Thy mighty ones to come down, O Lord. Let the heathen be wakened, and come up to the valley of Jehoshaphat: for there will I sit to judge all the heathen round about. Put ye in the sickle, for the harvest is ripe: come, get you down; for the press is full, the vats overflow; for their wickedness is great. Multitudes, multitudes in the valley of decision: for the day of the Lord is near in the valley of decision (Joel 3:11-14 KJV, emphasis added).

Wake up! You cannot go to battle while you sleep! The war cannot be won by a slumbering army.

It is time for a great awakening. While we've been asleep, God has been preparing and producing an army. As soldiers in the army of the Lord, we can no longer continue to push the snooze button. We must be attentive to the sound of the alarm. It is time to become alive and active with a renewed vision and purpose. Just as God took a valley full of disposed bones that were useless and lacking life to produce an army (see Ezek. 37), so does He desire to form an army of saints, devoted to a cause—the cause of Christ.

DEVOTED TO THE LORD

To become a member of an army above all else requires devotion. Devotion is being strongly attached or committed to a person or a cause. It is wholeheartedly supporting the person, beliefs, and vision you stand behind. It involves a high level of trust and loyalty. Someone who is devoted is not swayed by the winds of life and tossed about. It is someone who has his or her mind set straight on course. It is that person who does not look to the left or to the right but listens and obeys that Voice saying, "This is the way; walk in it" (Is. 30:21). It is that person who is willing to take up their cross and carry it for the sake of their own lives and others.

One of the greatest kings in the Bible, Kind David, knew the importance of having an army devoted to him. After defeating Goliath, David was sent by Saul to command an army of a thousand men. First Samuel 18:14 says, "In everything he did he had great success, because the Lord was with him." Over and over again throughout First and Second Samuel, we see where David and his men had great success. First Samuel 18:30 goes on to say, "The Philistine commanders continued to go out to battle, and as often as they did, David was met with more success than the rest of Saul's officers, and his name became well known." David was successful because he was devoted to the Lord had a heart for the Lord. David's men were devoted to him because he was a leader with good standing. Whether he was on the battlefield or finding refuge in a cave, his men were there. Whether he was pursuing or being pursued, they were by his side.

When it comes to serving the Lord, He looks for a heart of devotion. Second Chronicles 16:9 says, "For the eyes of the Lord range throughout the earth to strengthen those whose hearts are fully committed to Him."

Jesus was committed to the task set before Him. He was committed to the cost—even His own life. Thank the Lord He was committed to us. Are you committed to the cause of

Christ? Do you find yourself falling more and more in love with Him every day? Are you committed to do all He requires of you? Jesus gave His all for you; will you give your all for Him?

The soldiers of the United States of America live by a creed stating the beliefs that tie them together.

THE SOLDIERS CREED

I am an American Soldier.

I am a Warrior and member of a team.

I serve the people of the United States
and live the Army values.

I will always place the mission first.

I will never accept defeat.

I will never quit.

I will never leave a fallen comrade.

I am disciplined, physically and mentally tough,
trained and proficient in my warrior tasks and drills.

I always maintain my arms, my equipment and myself.

I am an expert and I am a professional.

I stand ready to deploy, engage, and destroy
the enemies of the United States
of America in close combat.

I am a guardian of freedom
and the American way of life.

I AM AN AMERICAN SOLDIER.[30]

Are we as devoted to the cause of Christ?

KNOWING THE COMMANDER

Are you doing great exploits for God? If not, I challenge you to look at the relationship you have with your heavenly Father. The answer lies in knowing Him.

There is a definite difference in knowing *about* Him and in *knowing* Him. Watching television about the lives of nationally known athletes does not mean that you "know them." Sure you might know all their stats and rankings, but that does not mean you have a personal relationship with them. The same applies to all those faces you see spread across the magazines when you are in a check-out line in the grocery store. Some people become so obsessed with tracking individuals' lives through the articles they read about them that they actually feel like they "know" them. This is an extremely false perception.

Knowing someone comes by developing a relationship through constant communication and time involved with that person. It comes with a level of trust that runs deep and escapes a notion of shallowness. Before Jesus was led to the Cross, He took time to pray for His followers. It was a prayer that emanated from the Father's heart.

> *And this is life eternal, that they might **know** Thee the only true God, and Jesus Christ, whom Thou has sent* (John 17:3 KJV, emphasis added).

In the Book of Philippians Paul states that he considers everything a loss compared to the greatness of knowing God. No matter who you are, God desires that you know Him. The disciples and men such as Paul, Silas, Timothy, Barnabas, and Stephen were able to do great exploits because they knew their God. Mark 3:14 reads,

> *And He ordained twelve, that they should be with Him, and that He might send them forth to preach, and to have power to heal sicknesses, and to cast out devils* (KJV).

In our own nightly meetings, we make it a priority to spend time with Him. He is what life is all about and what every church service should be about. As we take time to abide in Him and get to know Him, His presence is felt. He promises to be where two or more are gathered. He loves when we as a church worship Him and long to sit at His feet. The Holy Spirit comes where He is welcomed.

The Father sent His Son to the earth so that through Him, and Him alone, relationship would be restored to God. Furthermore, the Son sent the Spirit and the Spirit comes to reveal the Son. We can't know Jesus unless we have the indwelling Holy Spirit, but the Holy Spirit was not able to come until Jesus ascended into heaven. It was in His departing that the Holy Spirit was sent in His place to "reprove the world of sin, and of righteousness, and of judgment" and to guide us in all truth. One of the main reasons we meet together as a church is to allow the Holy Spirit to come so that we can get to know Jesus even more.

It is one thing to know the Word of God, but it is another thing to meet the God of the Word. Those who know Him will do great exploits. They too will have the power to heal sickness and cast out devils.

FULLY ARMED

To take our stand for righteousness and fight against the devil's schemes and the power of darkness, we must put on the armor of God and prepare for all that lies before us. Before you go into battle, you must make sure that you are armed, both defensively and offensively.

Ephesians 6:10-18 makes very clear those armor pieces that are necessary for the fight.

Finally, be strong in the Lord and in His mighty power. Put on the full armor of God so that you can take your stand against the devil's schemes. For our struggle is not against flesh and blood, but against the rulers, against the authorities, against the powers of this dark world and against the spiritual forces of evil in the heavenly realms. Therefore put on the full armor of God, so that when the day of evil comes, you may be able to stand your ground, and after you have done everything, to stand. Stand firm then with the belt of truth buckled around your waist, with the breastplate of righteousness in place, and with your feet fitted with the readiness that comes from the gospel of peace. In addition to all this, take up the shield of faith, with which you can extinguish all the flaming arrows of the evil one. Take the helmet of salvation and the sword of the Spirit, which is the word of God. And pray in the Spirit on all occasions with all kinds of prayers and requests. With this in mind, be alert and always keep praying for all the saints (Eph. 6:10-18).

After putting on this armor, the followers of Jesus Christ are required to fearlessly share the love of God with others.

Pray also for me, that whenever I open my mouth, words may be given me so that I will fearlessly make known the mystery of the gospel, for which I am an ambassador in chains. Pray that I may declare it fearlessly, as I should (Eph. 6:19-20).

As soldiers of the Cross, we need to realize that we are ambassadors for Christ. We need to pray that we will proclaim the mystery of the gospel without fear to the multitudes of those surrounding us.

We are soldiers who belong to the greatest army the world has ever seen or will ever see. No army on the face of this earth will ever compare to God's Army. As His frontline soldiers, you can hold fast to the promises He declares for you. The Bible is full of them. Take the truths in the sword of the Spirit and apply them to your lives. Pray the Word. Hide it in your heart. Its words are more valuable than any other gear you will ever wear; they are a lamp unto your feet and a light unto your path. God promises to light your every step.

STRONG SOLDIERS MUST HAVE A HEART

And he answering said, Thou shalt love the Lord thy God with all thy heart, and with all thy soul, and with all thy strength, and with all thy mind; and thy neighbor as thy-self. And He said unto him, Thou hast answered right: this do, and thou shalt live. But he, willing to justify himself, said unto Jesus, And who is my neighbor? And Jesus answering said, A certain man went down from Jerusalem to Jericho, and fell among thieves, which stripped him of his raiment, and wounded him, and departed, leaving him half dead. And by chance there came down a certain priest that way: and when he saw him, he passed by on the other side. And likewise a Levite, when he was at the place, came and looked on him, and passed by on the other side. But a certain Samaritan, as he journeyed came where he was: and when he saw him, he had compassion on him, And went to him, and bound up his wounds, pouring in oil and wine, and set him on his own beast, and brought him to an inn, and took care of him. And on the morrow when he departed, he took out two pence, and gave them to the host, and said unto him, Take care of him; and whatsoever thou spendest more, when I come again, I will repay thee. Which now of these three, thinkest thou, was neighbor unto him that fell among the thieves? And he said, He that showed mercy on him. Then said Jesus unto him, Go, and do thou likewise (Luke 10:27-37 KJV).

This is a story that you may have heard since childhood. It is a parable meant to teach life applications.

A man was on a journey from Jerusalem to Jericho, a distance of approximately 10 miles. We don't know exactly why he was on this journey, but the man was obviously on some sort of mission. While on this trip, he was overtaken by thieves who proceeded to strip him of everything but his very life. Left alone and helpless, the man had very little chance of survival.

Soon a priest came walking down this same road and stumbled across the severely beaten man. You would think that surely the priest, of all people, would stop to help this man. Surprisingly, the priest glanced him and thought it better to continue on his way.

A little while later, another man, a Levite, also passed by the man, decided to mind his own business, and continued on his journey as well. Finally, as a Samaritan man approached the victim, he stopped and took pity on the man. He tended to this man's wounds, carried him on his donkey to an inn, and continued to care for him, even up to the point where he paid for the man's living costs and anything extra that was required.

What was it that was so different about the Samaritan man from the priest and Levite? What is God trying to teach us here?

Notice the verses immediately before the parable. A man had been questioning Jesus regarding what he should do to have eternal life. Jesus responded by asking the man what the law books say. The man answered, "Love the Lord your God with all your heart and with all your soul and with all your strength and with all your mind, and love your neighbor as yourself." Wanting to teach this man exactly what the word "neighbor" meant, Jesus went on to tell the parable.

The Samaritan man had a genuine relationship with the Lord. He knew that God operated in love and was able to transform the love he had from the Father inside him onto others. It was not something the man had to conjure up. The gift of compassion was already present within him. God's very own nature of love seemed to envelope him. He couldn't help but express it and give it. In essence, Jesus was saying that anyone you meet is your neighbor. We are to love others as we love ourselves.

Are we like the priest who talks the talk but when we have the opportunity to share our faith, we do nothing? Or are we like the Levite who "minds his own business" and is just simply too busy and focused on ourselves to bother with anyone else? It is obvious that these two men had no heart of compassion for the lost.

I challenge you to strive to become more and more like the one who gave His life for you. May you too have a heart that is burdened for the hurting and lost. May you be so overwhelmed with the love of God that you in turn stop to give that love and life to others. May you be so pierced with the life-giving message that when you see a person wounded, hurting, needy, or desolate, you give them more than they could ever have asked for...Jesus.

BEGIN TO MOVE

You will never get anywhere if you don't start somewhere. While Jesus was on the face of this earth, He was a mover and a shaker. Wherever He went, He drew a crowd. There was hardly any place He could go that someone was not there with Him, except for when He went away to pray. He moved throughout the entire region touching and changing the lives He came across. He moved about His Father's business and left a lasting impression on countless lives, and continues to do so today.

Likewise, the disciples were not ones to sit around, especially after Jesus commissioned them. With the fresh anointing of the Holy Spirit, their lives were set ablaze as they moved forward with great joy at the task before them. Are you moving like the disciples did? Are you stepping into the calling that God has on your life? Are you sharing Him with others?

Nathan Cole, a farmer in the 1700s, paints a picture of the spiritual fervor that was alive and present in the New England states during his time. Allow this story to prompt you to pray for such a moving in America today.

> *Now it pleased God to send Mr. Whitefield into this land and my hearing of his preaching at Philadelphia, like one of the old apostles, and many thousands flocking after him to hear the gospel and great numbers converted to Christ, I felt the Spirit of God drawing me by conviction...Next I heard he was on Long Island and next at Boston and next at Northampton and then, one morning, all of a sudden, about 8 or 9 o'clock there came a messenger and said, 'Mr. Whitefield preached at Hartford and Wethersfield yesterday and is to preach at Middletown this morning at 10 o'clock. I was in my field, at work, I dropped my tool that I had in my hand and ran home and ran through my house and bade my wife get ready quick to go and hear Mr. Whitefield preach at*

Middletown and ran to my pasture for my horse with all my might, fearing I should be too late to hear him. I brought my horse home and soon mounted and took my wife up and went forward as fast as I thought the horse could bear, and when my horse began to be out of breath I would get down and put my wife in the saddle and bid her ride as fast as she could and not stop or slack for me except I bade her, and so I would run until I was almost out of breath and then mount my horse again, and so I several times to favour my horse...for we had twelve miles to ride double in little more than an hour.

On high ground I saw before me a cloud of fog rising, I first thought off from the great river but as I came nearer the road I heard a noise of something like a low rumbling of horses feet coming down the road and this cloud was a cloud of dust made by the running of horses' feet. It arose some rods in the air, over the tops of the hills and trees, and when I came within about twenty rods of the road I could see men and horses slipping along in the cloud like shadows and when I came nearer it was like a steady stream or horses and their riders, scarcely a horse more than his length behind another, all of a lather and some with sweat...We went down with the stream, I heard no man speak a word all the way, three miles, but everyone pressing forward in great haste, and when we got down to the old meetinghouse there was great multitude-it was said to be 3 or 4,000 people assembled together. We got off from our horses and shook off the dust, and the ministers were then coming to the meetinghouse. I turned and looked towards the great river and saw ferry boats running over loads of people, the oars rowed nimble and quick. Everything, men, horses and boats, all seemed to be struggling for life, the land and the banks over the river looked black with people and horses. All along the 12 miles I saw no man at work in his field but all seemed to be gone.[32]

No one was to be found. They all left the ordinary affairs of life and were on the move. Notice it was not a slow moving, but one of haste. People from everywhere, upon hearing that Whitefield would be holding a revival service, dropped what they were doing, because it was of unimportance, and moved to where he was.

Talk about hunger and desperation. People were in flight to make it there...and on time! Where is that vital tenacity needed in the church today? If people would move with the same enthusiasm they exhibit when they go see a movie, go to the mall, or go on vacation, America would look quite different. Someway, somehow America has lost its initial purpose for becoming a nation.

During the Puritan era, the separatists left England in search of this "New World" for religious freedom. Yes, they moved. They took a stand for righteousness and fought against the king of England and the powers of their dark world. They reacted. And because they fled and moved to this new land, freedom was established. But somewhere down the line, erosion has occurred. Our nation has lost its spiritual foundation.

BUT THE VICTORY IS OURS

Quitting and defeat are not an option. In Christ we are always victorious. That doesn't mean that we won't have obstacles and hurdles to face. That doesn't mean that the road to victory will be smooth or an easy ride. Storms will come. But we know that the One we have living in us is greater than he that lives in this world. We can walk through the storm and say, "Peace, be still," for we know that we are on the winning team.

Recorded in the Psalms, David sings these words to the Lord after being delivered from the hand of his enemies and from the hand of Saul:

It is God who arms me with strength and makes my way perfect. He makes my feel like the feet of a deer; He enables me to stand on the heights. He trains my hands for battle; my arms can bend a bow of bronze. You give me Your shield of victory, and Your right hand sustains me; You stoop down to make me great. You broaden the path beneath me, so that my ankles do not turn....He gives His king great victories; He shows unfailing kindness to His anointed, to David and his descendants forever (Ps. 18:32-36,50).

The righteous are never forsaken! The victory is ours!

Chapter Twenty

A SOLDIER FOR THE LORD

A vision is not seeing things as they are but as they will be. This is exactly how William Booth lived his life.

At a young age and after having lost his father, William experienced poverty and was deprived of any sense of a normal family life. Facing what seemed to be an existence filled with hopelessness, William rose to the occasion. As he witnessed the destitute and suffering all around him, he was bound to eradicate what he saw and do everything in his power to alter society.

Instead of feeling sorry for himself and his own situation, he chose to make a difference by focusing his attention on others. Personally experiencing life's hardships gave William a heart that beat for the lost and the needy, and became the seed which would later grow into what is now known as the Salvation Army.

As William Booth was faithful with the small, God began to make him master over much. The Salvation Army led a whole new advance for the Kingdom of God in that era. Instead of being a group that simply met together periodically for administration purposes, they literally lived up to their name. They were an army on a mission to bring salvation to the world and to do exactly what the Bible commanded—feed the poor, clothe the naked, care for the sick. They were the doers, and they acted on what they saw.

In James G. Lawson's book, *Deeper Experiences of Famous Christians*, he states, "While 'less creed and more deed' was the fundamental basis of Booth's Salvation Army, they did not neglect the great essential doctrines of repentance, faith, and necessity of holy living. To them repentance was not mere sorrow for sin, but real turning away from sin. Faith is not a mere intellectual act completed in a few seconds; but it is a real reliance of the soul upon Christ, beginning instantly but continuing through time and eternity.[32]

Being part of the Salvation Army required that a person be a passionate follower of Christ. Lukewarm living had no place there. James G. Lawson describes the members of the Salvation Army as being individuals who were required to be at their posts and to take part in every meeting if possible. Spiritual strength was required and General William Booth made sanctification, or the filling of the Holy Spirit, a fundamental doctrine of the Salvation Army. In many of the meetings that were held across the country, it was not an uncommon occurrence to see hundreds of people seeking salvation.[33]

General Booth's passion for the lost and needy continued to grow. His heart for the unsaved was so intense that he allowed nothing to prevent him from sharing the message of the gospel to those who were pushed to the side of societal bliss. Below describes a vision William saw while on one of his journeys. Reading this text reveals the fervor he felt for the lost.

> *On one of my recent journeys, as I gazed from the coach window, I was led into a train of thought concerning the condition of the multitudes around me. They were living carelessly in the most open and shameless rebellion against God, without a thought for their eternal welfare. As I looked out of the window, I seemed to see them all...millions of people all around me given up to their drink and their pleasure, their dancing and their music, their business and their anxieties, their politics and their troubles. Ignorant— willfully ignorant in many cases—and in other instances knowing all about the truth and not caring at all. But all of*

them, the whole mass of them, sweeping on and up in their blasphemies and devilries to the Throne of God. While my mind was thus engaged, I had a vision.

I saw a dark and stormy ocean. Over it the black clouds hung heavily; through them every now and then vivid lightning flashed and loud thunder rolled, while the winds moaned, and the waves rose and foamed, towered and broke, only to rise and foam, tower and break again.

In that ocean I thought I saw myriads of poor human beings plunging and floating, shouting and shrieking, cursing and struggling and drowning; and as they cursed and screamed they rose and shrieked again, and then some sank to rise no more.

And I saw out of this dark angry ocean, a mighty rock that rose up with its summit towering high above the black clouds that overhung the stormy sea. And all around the base of this great rock I saw a vast platform. Onto this platform, I saw with delight a number of the poor struggling, drowning wretches continually climbing out of the angry ocean. And I saw that a few of those who were already safe on the platform were helping the poor creatures still in the angry waters to reach the place of safety.

On looking more closely I found a number of those who had been rescued, industriously working and scheming by ladders, ropes, boats and other means more effective, to deliver the poor strugglers out of the sea. Here and there were some who actually jumped into the water, regardless of the consequences in their passion to "rescue the perishing." And I hardly know which gladdened me the most—the sight of the poor drowning people climbing onto the rocks reaching a place of safety, or the devotion and self-sacrifice of those whose whole being was wrapped up in the effort for their deliverance.

As I looked on, I saw that the occupants of that platform were quite a mixed company. That is, they were divided into different "sets" or classes, and they occupied themselves with different pleasures and employments. But only a very few of them seemed to make it their business to get the people out of the sea...But what puzzled me most was the fact that though all of them had been rescued at one time or another from the ocean, nearly everyone seemed to have forgotten all about it. Anyway, it seemed the memory of its darkness and danger no longer troubled them at all. And what seemed equally strange and perplexing to me was that these people did not even seem to have any care—that is any agonizing care—about the poor perishing ones who were struggling and drowning right before their very eyes...many of whom were their own husbands and wives, brothers and sisters and even their own children.

Now this astonishing unconcern could not have been the result of ignorance or lack of knowledge, because they lived right there in full sight of it all and even talked about it sometimes. Many even went regularly to hear lectures and sermons in which the awful state of these poor drowning creatures was described.

I have always said that the occupants of this platform were engaged in different pursuits and pastimes. Some of them were absorbed day and night in trading and business in order to make gain, storing up their savings in boxes, safes and the like.

Many spent their time in amusing themselves with growing flowers on the side of the rock, others in painting pieces of cloth or in playing music, or in dressing themselves up in different styles and walking about to be admired. Some occupied themselves chiefly in eating and drinking, others were taken up with arguing about the poor drowning creatures that had already been rescued.

But the thing to me that seemed the most amazing was that those on the platform to whom He called, who heard His voice and felt that they ought to obey it—at least they said they did—those who confessed to love Him much were in full sympathy with Him in the task He had undertaken—who worshipped Him or who professed to do so—were so taken up with their trades and professions, their money saving and pleasures, their families and circles, their religions and arguments about it, and their preparation for going to the mainland, that they did not listen to the cry that came to them from this Wonderful Being who had Himself gone down into the sea. Anyway, if they heard it they did not heed it. They did not care. And so the multitude went on right before them struggling and shrieking and drowning in the darkness.

And then I saw something that seemed to me even stranger than anything that had gone on before in this strange vision. I saw that some of these people on the platform whom this Wonderful Being had called to, wanting them to come and help Him in His difficult task of saving these perishing creatures, were always praying and crying out to Him to come to them!

Some wanted Him to come and stay with them, and spend His time and strength in making them happier. Others wanted Him to come and take away various doubts and misgivings they had concerning the truth of some letters He had written them. Some wanted Him to come and make them feel more secure on the rock—so secure that they would be quite sure that they should never slip off again into the ocean. Numbers of others wanted Him to make them feel quite certain that they would really get off the rock and onto the mainland someday: because as a matter of fact, it was well known that some had walked so carelessly as to loose their footing, and had fallen back again into the stormy waters.

So these people used to meet and get up as high on the rock as they could, and looking towards the mainland (where they thought the Great Being was) they would cry out, "Come to us! Come and help us!" And all the while He was down (by His Spirit) among the poor struggling, drowning creatures in the angry deep, with His arms around them trying to drag them out, and looking up—oh, so longingly but all in vain—to those on the rock, crying to them with His voice all hoarse from calling, "Come to Me! Come, and help Me!"

And then I understood it all. It was plain enough. The sea was the ocean of life—the sea of real, actual human existence. That lightning was the gleaming of piercing truth coming from Jehovah's Throne. That thunder was the distant echoing of the wrath of God. Those multitudes of people shrieking, struggling and agonizing in the stormy sea, was the thousands and thousands of poor harlots and harlot-makers, of drunkards and drunkard makers, of thieves, liars, blasphemers and ungodly people of every kindred, tongue and nation.

Oh what a black sea it was! And oh, what multitudes of rich and poor, ignorant and educated were there. They were all so unalike in their outward circumstances and conditions, yet all alike in one thing—all sinners before God—all held by, and holding onto, some iniquity, fascinated by some idol, the slaves of some devilish lust, and ruled by the foul fiend from the bottomless pit!

"All alike in one thing?" No, all alike in two things—not only the same in their wickedness but, unless rescued, the same in their sinking, sinking...down, down, down...to the same terrible doom. That great sheltering rock represented Calvary, the place where Jesus had died for them. And the people on it were those who had been rescued. The way they used their energies, gifts and time represented the occupations and amusements of those who professed to be saved from sin and hell—followers of the Lord Jesus Christ. The handful of fierce, determined ones, who were risking their own lives in saving the perishing were true soldiers of the cross of Jesus. That Mighty Being who was calling to them from the midst of the angry waters was the Son of God, "the

same yesterday, today and forever" who is still struggling and interceding to save the dying multitudes about us from this terrible doom of damnation, and whose voice can be heard above the music, machinery, and noise of life, calling on the rescued to come and help Him save the world.

My friends in Christ, you are rescued from the waters, you are on the rock, He is in the dark sea calling on you to come to Him and help Him. Will you go? Look for yourselves. The surging sea of life, crowded with perishing multitudes rolls up to the very spot on which you stand. Leaving the vision, I now come to speak of the fact—a fact that is as real as the Bible, as real as the Christ who hung upon the cross, as real as the judgment day will be, and as real as the heaven and hell that will follow it.

Look! Don't be deceived by appearances—men and things are not what they seem. All who are not on the rock are in the sea! Look at them from the standpoint of the great White Throne, and what a sight you have! Jesus Christ, the Son of God is, through His Spirit, in the midst of this dying multitude, struggling to save them. And He is calling on you to jump into the sea—to go right away to His side and help Him in the holy strife. Will you jump? That is, will you go to His feet and place yourself absolutely at His disposal?

A young Christian once came to me, and told me that for some time she had been giving the Lord her profession and prayers and money, but now she wanted to give Him her life. She wanted to go right into the fight. In other words, she wanted to go to His assistance in the sea. As when a man from the shore, seeing another struggling in the water, takes off those outer garments that would hinder his efforts and leaps to the rescue, so will you who still linger on the bank, thinking and singing and praying about the poor perishing souls, lay aside your shame, your pride, your cares about other people's opinions, your love of ease and all the selfish loves that have kept you back for so long, and rush to the rescue of this multitude of dying men and women.

Does the surging sea look dark and dangerous? Unquestionably it is so. There is no doubt that the leap for you, as for everyone who takes it, means difficulty and scorn and suffering. For you it may mean more than this. It may mean death. He who beckons you from the sea however, knows what it will mean—and knowing, He still calls to you and bids to you to come.

You must do it! You cannot hold back. You have enjoyed yourself in Christianity long enough. You have had pleasant feelings, pleasant songs, pleasant meetings, pleasant prospects. There has been much of human happiness, much clapping of hands and shouting of praises—very much of heaven on earth.

Now then, go to God and tell Him you are prepared as much as necessary to turn your back upon it all, and that you are willing to spend the rest of your days struggling in the midst of these perishing multitudes, whatever it may cost you.

You must do it. With the light that is now broken in upon your mind and the call that is now sounding in your ears, and the beckoning hands that are now before your eyes, you have no alternative. To go down among the perishing crowds is your duty. Your happiness from now on will consist in sharing their misery, your ease in sharing their pain, your crown in helping them to bear their cross, and your heaven in going into the very jaws of hell to rescue them. [34]

Was William Booth serious about what he preached? You better believe it.

Chapter Twenty-one

THE BEGINNINGS OF
AN AMERICAN AWAKENING

WHAT IS YOUR PASSION?

If I were to ask you what you are passionate about, what would your response be? Would it be football, soccer, basketball, or another sport? How about your hobbies? Are you a collector? Maybe you are passionate about your career and being successful. Some people are passionate about traveling; for others, is it eating. Whatever your passion, that is where you will spend most of your time.

Now consider this: Do any of those things have eternal significance?

What about souls? Are you as passionate for souls as you are for anything else?

What matters more than anything else in this world? Souls. But unfortunately, they rank very low in importance when considering where our time, money, and passions are spent.

Are you doing everything you possibly can to save the lives of the souls around you? If someone was about to hurt themselves or fall off a cliff, wouldn't you try everything in your power to save them?

I pray that God will birth in each and every person reading this book, a passion for the souls He has created and loves, and a desire to live a lifestyle of evangelism.

LIFESTYLE EVANGELISM

Lifestyle evangelism is exactly what it implies. Evangelism should be a lifestyle. It should not be something that takes place only on mission trips or city outreaches. It should be something that is part of your daily walk. We hold the gift of salvation that is to be readily given to anyone at any moment. If you were diagnosed with a terminal disease and someone had a cure, wouldn't you want him or her to immediately share the cure? So it is with the world. While the terminal disease of sin is eating away at them, we have the cure—Jesus Christ.

Passive evangelism doesn't work. We cannot use the excuse that we will share the gospel when we feel ready. Every day you pass by people who have most likely never heard that God loves them and has a wonderful plan for their life. You pass by people who are so mixed up in their beliefs and wish they knew the truth. You must tell them of the life that lives inside you. You must open your mouth. Fear cannot have its hold. You need to preach just for the simple fact that you don't know what the future holds for the person before you.

Don't make the mistake of failing to tell someone about Jesus when God stirs your heart. I waited too late to tell Frankie. I will never have that moment with him again. Life is about relationships, and you have all types of relationships with numerous people every day. Think about it. Every day you make contact with people you are familiar with—from the grocer to the banker, hairdresser, dry cleaner, restaurant server, gas station attendant, and on and on. Are you sharing the Good News with people you have built relationships? Are you sharing with people God brings across your path each day? Your life is of value to them because His life lives inside of you.

TESTIMONIES FROM THE REVIVALS

God's Word is comprised of numerous encounters when Jesus came face-to-face with all sorts of people. They ranged from the young to the old, the rich to the poor, the blind and lame to the strong, the humble to the proud. And with each soul He came in contact with, there was one common denominator. Each one had a dire need for a Savior. Each and every one needed Someone to see past their outward being, past the mistakes, past the disease, past the hurt, and to the heart of the inner man.

Once a soul is touched by the hand of God, a life is changed forever. An intimate experience with God propels a person forward with renewed vision and desire. God is alive and working in hearts this very hour and minute.

Joel 2:28-29 says, "I will pour out My Spirit on all people. Your sons and daughters will prophesy, your old men will dream dreams, your young men will see visions. Even on My servants, both men and women, I will pour out My Spirit in those days." Nothing is more amazing than watching the Spirit of God sweep over the young and old alike.

It is happening all now—the hand of God is touching countless individual lives who are hungry and desperate for Him. Following are testimonies of the many who continue to flood the services of our ministry as God is moving with a fresh sense of His Spirit on His people.

- A pastor, while on an outreach ministry, walked into the middle of a softball game, halted the play, and led the entire team to the Lord as they joined hands in the middle of the field.

- A girl, 16 years of age, after having a vision of a man sitting on a park bench, went out after the outreach, looking for the man. She and some friends, while searching for the man, stopped at five different city parks, witnessing the salvation of 10 people before they found the man they were looking for. He was on a park bench and prayed to receive Christ for the first time.

• During our Seattle crusade, some individuals tried to convince two girls that they would be better off not coming to the services. Instead of listening to their advice, the girls followed their heart and made their way to the arena where our services were being held. While there, the girls were saved. A few weeks after the meeting, I received a call informing me that one of the girls was killed in a car accident on Tacoma's Narrows Bridge.

• In a trailer park in New Jersey, two people—at two separate locations and times—came to know the Lord. Later, it was discovered that those two people were a son and his mother who had not talked to each other in more than 10 years. A restoration of their lives began immediately.

• Our team and others when on an outreach unexpectedly came upon a husband and wife in two completely different sections of a city on the very same day. They both gave their lives to Jesus.

• While witnessing in a mall, our team and others met up with a fiancée on one side of the mall and the soon-to-be groom on the other side. They both were saved right before their wedding day.

• During a service, a team member and some youth were sent to find a man at a neighboring hotel who had called on the phone because he needed the Lord. Upon arriving at the hotel, not only did the team see the man on the phone get saved; but two young people, the desk clerk, the bartender, and the coach of an athletic team staying in the hotel received the gift of salvation as well. The place was stirred!

- A very shy girl came to one of our services, where God touched her mightily, and she gave overwhelmingly in the offerings. In a short time, she led her first souls to Christ—six in one day. She then was blessed with a new job that tripled her salary. One morning, as she was running late for work, she passed by a girl on the highway. The Lord quickened her to stop, but she ignored the prompting. She then made a wrong turn and saw the girl again. The Lord nudged her again. After a second wrong turn, she saw the girl a third time. The Lord said, "*Go now!*" and she did. She pulled off to the side of the road and led her in the sinner's prayer. As the girl received Christ, she looked up with tears streaming down her face and said, "Thank you for stopping me. You see, my friends were killed in a horrific car accident on this road, and I was supposed to be in the car. You didn't know this; but just before you stopped me, I was going to walk in front of a bus and kill myself." Thank the Lord that the "shy" girl endured a tough message in revival and let God use her!

- While eating at a Bennigan's in Florida, we witnessed the trembling anointing fall on a waitress. She began to shake as she confessed that her pastor had raped her. Her pastor also happened to be her father. She was gloriously saved.

- A young man who was about to throw himself over a bridge was saved that same day.

- A man in desperation prayed, "Lord, if You are out there, I need You today, or I will take my life!" That very day he met a Holy Ghost-filled woman who shared with Him the love of Jesus.

- An owner of a store who needed a healing came to me. I prayed for her while everyone in the store watched. She was instantly healed, and the people saw the power of God.

- A man in Michigan was set free from heavy drug use after one church service. The Lord gave me a word for him: "Within six months, you'll be in full-time ministry." It came to pass, and he is in ministry to this very day where God is using him to shake his own region.

- A man with a terminal heart condition was healed in a Michigan parking lot!

- In New Jersey, the entire population at a day camp was preached to and 37 people accepted the Lord.

- Universities are great places to reach young people! Once, we stopped a group of prospective students touring a campus. At first, they thought we were part of the registration process, and allowed us to talk to them. Many of them were radically saved.

- As I was praying, God showed me that there was a man at an Applebee's restaurant who needed salvation. The Lord impressed upon me the urgency for this man to hear God's message immediately. So in the middle of the service, I sent a team out to find him. One hour later, at midnight, the man was sitting in his first church service filled with the glory of God.

These testimonies continue to happen as we travel the regions. God is awesome!

TESTIMONIES FROM WISCONSIN

- While we were ministering in Wisconsin, God awoke one pastor and gave him three words for an old high school friend whom he hadn't seen in years. Obeying God, he went looking for his friend at his house and place of work, but he was not at either place. On his way home, the pastor drove over a hill and came to a stop sign. While waiting for his turn to proceed, another car came over the hill and coasted to a stop right next to the pastor. The man had just run out of gas. And what do you know?...it was the man the pastor had been looking for. He told the man what God had said, and the man was gloriously saved. Glory to God!

• One lady, witnessed to in a mall, declined the invitation for salvation. Trying to dismiss what she had heard, she walked to the other side of the mall. But again, she met another team member in the ministry, and this time she was saved. Following her own salvation, she led most of her coworkers to Jesus. Currently, she has led over 100 people to the Lord. She has never attended a new believer's class or a soul-winning class, but that hasn't kept her from sharing the Good News!

• A 10-year-old girl was touched and led the manager of Subway to Jesus while she made her sandwich and while many were in line waiting...and listening.

• One night during a service, I asked those people to come forward for prayer who were experiencing an urgent family situation. A married lady came forward to pray for her husband. She had planned on leaving him the next morning. God spoke to me to call him on his cell phone right then and there. In the middle of the service, I had an opportunity to lead him to Jesus as the church was praying for his soul. He broke down over the phone, and the divorce was cancelled.

• In the middle of another service, God showed me four people at a Target who needed Him. It was a matter of urgency. And so, teams were immediately sent out. Approximately 10 miles away, two young men who had just been arrested and their two friends were saved in the parking lot. They drove immediately to the church for more prayer.

• Unexpectedly, while having a special pastors' meal after the service, God showed us He wasn't done moving on our hearts. The power of God fell, and we all were on our faces until 1:30 AM.

- Two miraculous healings of partially blind people have occurred. Tumors have dissolved. The lame have walked.

TESTIMONIES FROM ANCHORAGE, ALASKA

- While in Anchorage, Alaska, we saw approximately 1000 people saved in 10 days!

- One night teams were sent out to four different locations. Nineteen people were saved during the service. Another night, the deafening cries of the crowd lasted until 5:00 AM. Three hours later, with no night's sleep, they hit the streets of downtown Anchorage and won 140 souls.

ADVENTURES WITH GOD

In the street outreaches, we teach and train believers to yield and rely on the supernatural. If the anointing is real and God's power can overwhelm us in services, then it should work on the streets as well. We encourage believers to pray for the sick and cast out devils—in public—from Wal-Marts to 7-11s, restaurants to schools, beaches to parks. We have seen the awesome power of heaven being poured out in a glorious way. Here are a few more stories of our adventures with God.

My crusade director and I decided to take a couple hours off during a New Jersey revival to go play golf. We were cruising down the highway when suddenly, we saw a woman at an intersection fall into the street at a bus station. My friend said that he saw what looked like a demon push this woman in the back. Just then, a bus pulled up to the station.

I immediately drove across the intersection, cutting off rapidly moving cars and cursing drivers, and pulled up behind the bus. I jumped out of my car and ran up to this woman who was already surrounded by three people including the bus driver. I noticed that she had gone into a grand mal seizure right there on the highway. Her face was pounding into the cement, and someone had put a piece of cardboard under her head to protect her from tearing up her face. The cardboard was soon full of blood as the three people looked around helplessly.

The world does not know what to do in crisis because they have no power. I took over and said, "Stand back. I am a preacher. God will help this woman." I laid my hands on her as she was banging into the pavement. I commanded that the devil leave her body in Jesus' name. Within seconds she stopped, and a total peace came over her. By this time, all the passengers on the bus were watching. I want you to know I didn't feel any particular anointing. I was standing on a highway in New Jersey in my golf gear. I didn't have the worship band playing the perfect song. I didn't even have the intercessory group praying to heaven. God is bigger than those things. He is just looking for someone to stop and be used.

After our meetings, people often are filled with a new excitement to share their faith with others. Some haven't shared in years, and others have never shared at all. There have been times that we have literally stopped cars and flagged people down in an effort to preach to them. And what do we find? That people are hungry and open to the gospel. Some have broken down in tears. Some have even pulled over and asked, "What must I do to be saved?" Teenagers all across Wisconsin have literally run after cars to tell them the Good News. We've come to call it a Holy Ghost traffic jam. As we stopped one car, other vehicles were forced to stop behind them. We then proceeded to minister to all the passengers. Sometimes we got into their vehicles with them. One witness jumped into a truck with a family, and the entire family was so ready and ripe, they broke down in the car. We have even been pulled over by police officers who were called out to check on us. Unbeknown to them, God was drawing them also, and many officers in America have been saved. One policeman told us, "I cannot believe this. I came to check on a disturbance, and I ended up giving my heart to Jesus!" That's how it should be. Glory to God!

One of the most likely times we see people saved is when the nightly services are over. As we adjourn in the wee morning hours, we find ourselves sitting in restaurants staring directly into the eyes of people who have no concept of the God who created them. As we sit there, so full of what we have just received in the meeting not an hour before, we can't help but share. We have seen many waitresses converted, some who have been overcome by God's power standing right there at the table. Others have broken down in tears, jumped up and down, and even been baptized in the Holy Ghost. One day, two waitresses were saved, filled with the Holy Spirit, and spoke in other tongues in an Olive Garden.

THE HOLY SPIRIT'S FOLLOW-UP

As we practice sharing Jesus with those around us, we have often been criticized in regard to our methods of follow-up. In each church we have ministered, there have been hundreds to thousands of individual lives who have come into contact with a person sharing the gospel on the streets. Considering all the individual lives getting saved, we realize that there are what we would call "baby Christians" out there who need to be discipled, and the majority of churches that we minister in make it a point to contact those individuals with a follow-up letter, or even a Bible.

All too often though there are people who are quick to criticize our lack of follow-up without first realizing what is taking place. I believe that we have underestimated the power of the Holy Spirit when it comes to follow-up. Each person who is confronted with the gospel has a decision to make—to either accept Him or reject Him. In that same aspect, he or she has another choice to make, and that is to either choose to develop their walk with the Lord and pursue a place of fellowship or to allow themselves to slide back into their previous condition. If a person is genuine in their conversion, there will be an appetite there for the things of God. There will be a realization of the significance of God in their lives.

As Jesus ministered in the New Testament, the lives that were touched by God were truly touched. Once a person is touched, he knows it. I highly doubt he could stay out of His presence. Yet, I don't believe that Jesus made it a primary factor to go back and trace over His steps making sure that each person who heard the Word received it and held on to it. Was this His hope? Certainly. Yet He had to believe that the seed planted on the "good soil" hearts would produce much. He clearly stated that there were four groups of people who would hear or receive the gospel, and three would produce no fruit.

As believers our main commission is in sharing the gospel. We believe in the Word of God, and the bottom line is that the same people who criticize us would have a hard time with Jesus. In the end, His church numbered 120. Of all the thousands and thousands and thousands who were healed and restored and ministered to, from blind eyes seeing to deaf ears hearing, only 120 stayed in "His Church." And only another 350 saw Him after He died. Yet He had to believe that what was spoken to them would take root. Again, we believe in follow-up; however, Jesus placed the emphasis on preaching the Kingdom of God. Three examples are the woman at the well, the Ethiopian eunuch, and the prison guard in Acts 16 when Paul and Silas experienced a great earthquake. They were not contacted by man again and again; however, I am sure the Lord "followed up" on His own children.

On one occasion, a pastor came up to me with a smirk spread across his face, ready to somehow degrade our method of outreach. He asked, "How many souls that you all have won have actually come into this church?" (as if that was the basis for salvation). I responded, "Pastor, I don't know. I apologize. I don't know how many who come into the church actually get saved, but I do know this: One hundred percent of the people we don't talk to will go to hell." In no way was I trying to undermine him, but I wanted him to see the importance of reaching out to the multitudes and wiping the blood off our hands.

TELL THE WORLD CRUSADES

In the year 2000, we conducted our first Tell the World Crusade in Seattle. Since then, the ministry has held a crusade every year. In 2001 we went to New Jersey, 2002 Michigan, and in 2003 Wisconsin. Currently we believe God is moving on the hearts of those in the New England states where our country was born. Our prayer is that this precious nation that was grounded on the principals of the Word will return to God wholeheartedly. Pray for us as we continue carrying this message to a world in desperate need of Him.

Seattle 2000

For our Seattle area crusade, we had planned the event "Tell the World" for seven months and rented the largest arena in the county, which could hold six thousand people. Although several local churches had offered their assistance, there were some church leaders who approached me asking us to cancel the crusade. Their reason—they said they weren't ready. The Lord, by the Spirit, spoke through me and I said to them, "You're not ready, but guess Who is?" The harvest is white and ripe. The world is dying and going to hell. Their churches had been in existence and established for 30 years, and they still weren't ready. What had they been doing for all those 30 years? The Lord showed me that when the harvest is ready, it is only ripe for a season. We must act according to the time of the harvest, not when it suits the harvesters.

The Lord told us to pray for laborers—harvesters. While some churches weren't ready, others joined hands. People were touched and crowds grew up to 1,200 people a night. We had a great 10-day event where 1,500 people were converted. Miraculous healings of people who were terminally ill were reported in the local newspapers. Over $100,000 in finances were donated for the event. At that particular time, it was everything it was supposed to be. On the surface, it had been successful. However, when all was said and done, I took time and examined the crusade very closely, and I realized overall that it was just a typical

American event that happens in cities all over the country. Great word, great turnout, lives touched. And then I thought, *Does America need more events like this?*

My heart started to break. I realized our results may have communicated success to the American church, but my heart longed for more. I knew that America didn't need another good event; America needed an awakening. That area hadn't really been shaken with the presence of God. In fact, months after I left, the area was almost completely unaffected.

America needs more—a lot more. In the early part of 2001 I began to cry out for that more, and a spirit of prayer came upon me. Every day for two to three hours, I began to cry out on my face to God for something more to happen in this land.

New Jersey 2001

This was the year that the Lord spoke to me and called me back to my hometown area in New Jersey, because revival would break out that summer. We began planning "Tell the World 2001" to be held in a tent on the New Jersey shore, and I was determined that the one place I would never set the tent up was on my home church's land.

For eight months, we planned the event and still had no land. Five days before the event, I arrived in New Jersey—still no land for the tent. What did I do? I called my home pastor, and sure enough, within hours we had a permit to put up the tent on his property. Once again, the plans and preparations for the event were going smoothly. Meetings were to close by 10:00 PM each night to adhere to the noise restrictions. However, after just two weeks, certain circumstances led to the police coming and the pastor deciding to close the meetings. He announced that we could have one last service, but it would have to be held in their new sanctuary. I continued to trust the word of the Lord that revival would break out.

That night, the Spirit of God came. All nine gifts of the Spirit manifested; people laughed, cried, wept, danced, shouted, ran, jumped, and remained silent. The service lasted almost eight hours! They had to carry me back to my hotel room. The next day we realized something special had happened, so we had another service. The same thing happened again. We decided to continue the meetings. God knew that what needed to happen could not happen in a tent outside. He needed free reign to do whatever He desired. You cannot put God in a box. These meetings continued for three and one-half months.

The night services consisted of crying out to heaven, and sometimes they lasted until almost 4:00 AM. Occasionally, bus-loads of people would arrive at midnight. And during the day-time, we hit the streets preaching boldly. We flooded the Jersey Shore boardwalks with the glory of heaven, and over 6,000 people were converted. Over 100 ministers from many different states came to see the revival of souls. God had set up the Book of Acts pattern for us—cry out, go out, and give out. Whatever He gives to us, He expects us to give out. Freely we have received, freely we must give. A true revival broke out in New Jersey that year. It was the beginning of what the Lord was about to do in America.

Michigan 2002

We knew something special had happened in New Jersey, but then, the Lord took us to the state of Michigan. There, the same things began happening. One day, a Christian school decided to close, and they went out witnessing. Many were saved right in their driveways. They couldn't believe young people were preaching the truth of the gospel while they should have been at school. We realized New Jersey was amazing, but it had affected only one church for eternity. We knew the Lord wanted to touch entire regions.

In Michigan, we again met with leadership, and many were excited. I soon found out, though, that anyone can get excited for a while, but when persecution and affliction arise for the Word's sake, many stumble. Anyone can shout hallelujah or amen on

Sunday morning, but how many will continue to shout the other six days, for week after week, month after month, year after year?

It was in Michigan where we came across religious leaders who were more passionate about their board meetings and luncheons than the harvest. Irregardless, 11,000 people were converted in Michigan. Forty-four of those were walk-up conversions—people who walked up to the dome out of curiosity and were radically saved. It made the front papers of all the local newspapers and appeared on television news broadcasts. One station even came and did their morning show live from the air dome. The power of God manifested in stores, malls, parks, and school grounds. People even got saved at the urinals! We were there for almost one year.

It was in Michigan that the Lord did the greatest work in me. I truly died there. After three years of ministry I had finally died to myself. "Unless a seed falls to the ground and dies, it cannot spring forth life." God told us to stay in a city where so many now wanted us to leave. Churches whose congregations had exploded were now asking us to get out of town. It was a "My God, why have You forsaken me?" experience.

After Michigan, we cried out to heaven again. We were looking for hungry leaders—pastors who were tired of boardroom diplomacy and truly wanted to experience revival at any costs. At that time, I was about to quit and give up. Just three years into this ministry, I thought, *How can I even deal with this?* The church world seemed like a zoo, and it wasn't until I left for Tampa, Florida that God healed my heart.

I realized that Jesus' toughest fight was with the religious people. How it must have hurt Him. As His follower, I must do the same and endeavor to love the world and shake up the religious. I had been quoted as saying that I would never endure another "Michigan"; however, knowing what I know now, I would do it all over again. It's at those times that the Lord really shapes you and builds the things in you that you will need for the rest of the way. That Michigan crusade made me who I am today and prepared me for what I will walk in tomorrow.

Wisconsin 2003

Stepping out in ministry, we continued to pray that the Lord would send us to serious pastors who would be willing to do anything for revival. An evangelist friend of mine recommended that I call a man in Dodgeville, Wisconsin. Following his advice, I called this pastor, and he asked me when I could come. Although I told him I could come around the holidays, he said that many of his members worked extra hours at the main plant during the holiday season. However, by the end of the conversation he said, "We are so hungry for God; come at that time anyway." So we were on our way to Dodgeville, Wisconsin.

While there, God swept Dodgeville for four weeks and heaven came down. Over 300 people were converted in the streets. People were repenting on Main Street of downtown Dodgeville! We then asked if there were more hungry pastors in the area and discovered a pastor in Janesville. Before we knew it, we were in Janesville watching over 600 salvations being recorded in four weeks.

One girl broke down in the mall and gave her heart to the Lord. Three days later, on a Sunday, she came to her new pastor with 10 decision cards for people she had led to the Lord. Although we had been asked to leave the mall, God was still to have His way. She worked there and had continued to win souls. In four weeks, she had led over 100 people to Christ! We then realized something was happening that we had never seen before. The fire of God was sweeping the state as revivals were held all over the place. Thousands upon thousands were getting saved.

We had been given a word that when we came to Milwaukee it would explode with revival, and it did. In the first church we attended, over 3,000 people were saved in three weeks. Teenagers were crying out like I had never seen before. Meetings would go until the early hours of the morning. Pastors and leaders were hungry and winning souls themselves. One night I closed the meeting early at 1:00 AM, but several youth from another church decided they weren't done crying out. They asked their youth pastor to open their sanctuary so they could continue pouring their hearts out to heaven. In the daytime, kids were witnessing with abandonment, chasing down cars, preaching boldly at school and in their neighborhoods. Some were having visions of people in malls and would go and see those same people they envisioned get gloriously converted. New converts were getting saved in Olive Garden and moments later being filled with the Spirit and speaking in other tongues right at the table!

Over 35,000 people were converted in 2003, with many more still happening today. The last 20 churches we ministered in we had seen more people saved in a few weeks than in the entire history of their churches. We started with 30 salvations the first night and went up to 5,000 in the end. God truly worked wonders in Wisconsin. On just one day, 1,700 people were converted!

I will always remember two things about that revival. One night I was laying prostrate on the stage in a church. I had been preaching all night and had taught on the offering for an hour. I noticed that the adults had seemed to tune me out, but the young people were following along. Later that night, at about 2:30 AM, I looked up and saw several youth crying out—not one or two, but dozens and dozens all over the building crying out in desperate travail for heaven.

One young girl about five years old caught my attention. Her face was in utter agony, yet the most beautiful picture of desperation I had ever seen, as she was crying, "Jesus, Jesus, Jesus." This happened close to seven and one-half hours into the service. She was in another realm as she was weeping between the porch and the altar. It was awesome.

The second thing I will never forget was the next to the last night in the air dome. That day, 700 people were saved, and many groups from other states were going home. After the service, a group of young people came over to me outside the dome and said, "Brother Tommie, will you agree with us for tomorrow?" I said, "Yes, what would you like to agree for?" They said, "We are believing for 1000 people to get saved tomorrow." I almost chuckled, thinking there was no way that would ever happen. However, I didn't want to discourage the simple faith of these kids, ages 8, 12, 14, and 16, and so, I gathered with them and prayed. God knew the desire of their hearts.

I went home and again asked the Lord to grant them their request. I prayed, "Lord, I have been saved most of my life. I have never even asked You for that. Please open blind eyes, open deaf ears. Do whatever You need to, but meet these kids in a special way." The next night the place went crazy as I announced that almost 1,100 souls were saved! May we all have that kind of passion for the lost!

Boston 2004

Already something is happening in New England. If any part of America is indicative of what has happened to our church and our nation, it is by far New England. This place where Puritans and Pilgrims once came to seek the Father earnestly, now has become the seat of liberalism. On grounds once set apart as Bible schools, perverted thinking and secular humanism abound. The area overflows with witchcraft, homosexual lifestyles, and self-help groups. Statistics show that only six percent of the New England population is saved, a nationwide low. The average evangelical church numbers 70 people, again a nationwide low. No area has drifted so far away from God as this. But the Lord told us that something would happen in Boston during the year 2004. I believe that the spirit of Jonathan Edwards is being rekindled once again in the New England area. The Boston Crusade ended up ushering in a whole new revolution even greater than what we could ever explain. A revolution that would eventually shock the world. A revolution that would thrust this ministry ahead with renewed vision for this nation as a whole. The timing could not have been perfect as we were holding meetings at the exact time as the Democratic National Convention. Hundreds upon thousands of people met in the city for the purpose of supporting or protesting the event. Boston was flooded with people. Among the flood were followers of Jesus Christ who dispersed themselves throughout the city from downtown to Harvard, to the T-Station's and the convention grounds. The testimonies were unreal. A genuine revolution is beginning. It is beginning in the heart of the believer to step it up a notch as it is beginning in the heart of the new born again believer that there is another way of living, and it is living the life that God calls you to live.

What's to Come

When we held our citywide crusade in Wisconsin, we were privileged to set up our air dome on the grounds of the Milwaukee Brewers' new stadium. Our 2000-seat air dome was planted right next to the 50,000-seat stadium. It pictured where we were headed.

Soon stadiums will be filled with extended revival meetings. Whole regions will become aflame. The church will not be stuck inside buildings and conference or seminar rooms. We will invade the streets of every city in America. A great revolution is happening as we speak. This is not just theory. This is happening.

The Lord spoke to me and said, "Have the people pay a price for the glory. Allow the fire to come down upon the sacrifice. Preach as tough a message as you can handle to preach. Pierce the religion out of people. Love them into their fullness. I have so much more for them. Then I will fill their houses with the glory. Instruct them and teach them and get them to 'take the glory to the gate called Beautiful.'" Even today as you read, people are taking the the glory to the gate called Beautiful. Not one miracle recorded in the New Testament ever happened in a church; they occurred in public places. The world is waiting for the manifestation of the sons of God to appear.

Recently, I visited two historic places in America. The first was Salem, Massachusetts. Salem was the place of the first church in America, a central place of Puritanism. It has now become the seat of witchcraft. This city amazed me. We then went to Provincetown, Massachusetts, at the tip of Cape Cod. This is where the Mayflower Compact was written. It states that the land was dedicated for the glory of God and the furtherance of the Christian faith. Now the land has become a den of iniquity as it is the seat of homosexuality in the northeast. As I visited both places, I realized that the spiritual condition of our country can be blamed on the sleeping church. The light has been hid under the bushel. The fear of men has gripped us and closed our mouths. And now we have to deal with the fruits of our own lack of labor. We haven't worked the land, and the land is now desolate.

But...I believe a fresh wind is blowing. Heaven is beginning to get a hold on us. There is a stirring of passion and a distaste for hypocrisy. The true church is rising. Saints, it's time to make full proof of our life and ministry. Do your best for Him while you can. He is worthy. He is worth every bit of humiliation. He is worth dying for. It doesn't matter what the world thinks; it matters what He thinks. This life is a vapor, but we will spend eternity with Him. Go and do for your Father. We must awaken now.

As He died to make men holy, let us live to make men free. His truth is marching on. *Get ready America, here comes your church!*

THE SOULWINNING SCRIPT

Hi, my name is (*your name*). What's your name?

[*Their name*], I've got to tell you two things real quick—that God loves you and has a wonderful plan for your life. Before I go, let me ask you a real quick question. If you were to die today, do you know for sure, without a shadow of a doubt, that you would go straight to heaven?

[If the answer is "no," or, "I think so," continue with the script. If the answer is "yes," say, "Great, why would you say yes?" If they do not say, "I have Jesus in my heart/born again," go with the script.]

Let me tell you three things the Bible says. Number one: It says, "For **all** have sinned and come short of the glory of God." Number two: It says, "The wages of sin is death, but the **gift** of God is eternal life through Jesus Christ our Lord." And number three: It says, "For **whosoever** shall call upon the name of the Lord shall be saved." And you're a "whosoever," right? Of course, you are. We all are. Before I go, I'm going to say a quick prayer for you...just bow your head and close your eyes.

Lord, I pray that You bless [*their name*] and his/her family with long and healthy lives. Make Yourself so real to him/her. And if [*their name*] has never received Jesus Christ as his/her Lord and Savior, I pray he/she will do so right now.

[*Their name*], if you would like to receive Jesus Christ as your Lord and Savior, just say this after me...

Dear Lord Jesus—Come into my heart.—Forgive me of my sins.—Wash me.—Cleanse me.—Change me.—Fill me with Your Holy Spirit and set me free.—Jesus, I believe You died for my sins—and are coming back again for me.—Give me a passion for the lost—a hunger for the things of God—and a holy boldness.—Help me to fulfill—all that You have called me to do.—I thank You that I'm now forgiven — and on my way to heaven. — In Jesus' name. Amen.

[*Their name*], I have some good news for you. As a minister of the gospel of Jesus Christ, I tell you today that all your sins are forgiven right now! Remember, if you make a mistake, don't run from God. Run to Him because He loves you and has a wonderful plan for your life.

ENDNOTES

Chapter One

1. Merriam Webster Dictionary Online: http://www.m-w.com/dictionary.htm.

Chapter Four

2. Merriam Webster Dictionary Online: http://www.m-w.com/dictionary.htm.

3. Merriam Webster Dictionary Online: http://www.m-w.com/dictionary.htm.

Chapter Five

4. Whitefield, George. "Marks of a True Conversion." *Christian News*. 8 Dec. 2003. http://www.worthynews.com/sermons/whitfield_trueconversion.htm.

Chapter Six

5. Unknown. "Jonathan Edwards, 1703-1758, Bible Scholar, Preacher." *CNN Beliver's Web* 17 Mar. 2003. http://www.believersweb.net/view.cfm?ID=118.

6. Hosier, Helen K. *Heros of Faith: Jonathan Edwards: The Great Awakener* (Uhrichsville, OH: Barbour Publishing Inc.), 95.

Chapter Nine

7. Steve Miller, *Extreme Journey Get More Out of It:* (Nashville, TN: Thomas Nelson Publishers 2001).

Chapter Ten

8. Unknown. "Biography of Martin Luther." 24 Oct 2003. http://www.sacklunch.net/biography/L/MartinLuther.html.

9. Unknown. "Biography of Martin Luther" 24 Oct 2003. http://www.sacklunch.net/biography/L/MartinLuther.html.

10. Ruckman "Martin Luther, 1483-1546, German Reformer." *Believers Web* CCN. 17 Mar. 2003. http://www.believersweb.net/view.cfm?ID 124.

11. Murray, Lain. "Jonathan Edwards, 1703-1758: Revival in America Part 2." *The Heath Christian Bookshop.* http//www.christian-bookshop.co.uk/free/biogs/jed2.htm.

12. Unknown. "Jonathan Edwards, 1703-1758, Bible Scholar, Preacher." *Believers Web CCN.* 17 March 2003. 8 Jan 2004. http://www.believersweb.net/view.cfm?ID118.

13. Hosier, Helen K. *Heros of Faith: Jonathan Edwards: The Great Awakener* (New Kensington, PA: Whitaker House, 1998),79-81.

14. Whitefield, George. "Marks of a True Conversion." *Christian News.* 8 Dec 2003. http://www.worthynews.com/sermons/whitfield_trueconversion.htm.

15. Wesley, John. "Sermon 141<text from the 1872> On the Holy Spirit." 24 Oct 2003. http://www.raptureme.com/resource/wesley/serm_141.html.

16. Finney, Charles G. "The Autobiography of Charles G. Finney-Birth and Early Education." *Biographies-Christians Unite.* 14 Nov 2003. http://bible.christiansunite.com/charles_ finney/finney01.shtml.

17. Finney, Charles G. "The Autobiography of Charles G. Finney-Birth and Early Education." *Biographies-Christians Unite.* 14 Nov 2003. http://bible.christiansunite.com/charles_ finney/finney01.shtml.

18. Tozer, A.W. *The Pursuit of God: The Human Thirst for the Divine* (Camp Hill, PA: Christian Publications) Chapter 4. http//www.worldinvisible.com/library/tozer/5f00.0888/5f00.088 8.04.htm.

19. Finney, Charles G. "The Autobiography of Charles G. Finney-Conversion to Christ." *Biographies-Christians Unite.* 24 Oct 2003. http://bible.christiansunite.com/charles_finney/finney02.shtml.

20. Finney, Charles G. "The Autobiography of Charles G. Finney-Conversion to Christ." *Biographies-Christians Unite*. 24 Oct 2003. http://bible.christiansunite.com/charles_finney/finney02.shtml.

21. Finney, Charles G. "The Autobiography of Charles G. Finney-Conversion to Christ." *Biographies-Christians Unite*. 24 Oct 2003. http://bible.christiansunite.com/charles_finney/finney02.shtml.

22. Finney, Charles G. *Holy Spirit Revivals: How You Can Experience the Joy of Living in God's Power* (New Kensington, PA: Whitaker House, 1999).

23. Unknown. "Evan Roberts and the Welsh Revival of 1904." 3 Dec 2003. *The Heath Christian Bookshop* http://www.christian-bookshop.com.uk/free/ biogs/roberts3.htm.

Chapter Eleven

24. Merriam Webster Dictionary Online: http://www.m-w.com/dictionary.htm.

25. Wigglesworth, Smith. Book by Author Albert Hibert, *The Secret of His Power* (Tulsa, OK: Harrison House 1982), 103.

Chapter Twelve

26. Unknown. "Evan Roberts." *The Watchword Newsletter* Vol. 25. 24 Oct 2003. http://www.sendrevival.com/history/welsh_revival/evan_roberts_brief.htm.

27. Wesley, John paraphrased. "The Impact of Influence by Pastor Glenn Pease" 25 Oct. 2004. http//:www.faithmania.com/glenn-pease-article-influence.html.

Chapter Fifteen

28. Lewis, C.S. *Mere Christianity* (Nashville, TN: Broadman and Holman Publishers, 1980), 118.

29. Hibbert, Albert. *The Secrets of His Power* (Tulsa, OK: Harrison House, 1982), 74.

Chapter Nineteen

30. American Soldier Creed. http://basic.armystudyguide.com/general/Soldiers-Creed.htm. Free resource provided by www.ArmyStudyGuide.com.

31. Hosier, Helen K. *Heros of the Faith: Jonathan Edwards: The Great Awakener* (Uhrichsville, OH: Barbour Publishing Inc.), 85-87.

Chapter Twenty

32. Lawson, James G. *Deeper Experiences of Famous Christians* (New Kensington, PA: Whitaker House, 1998), 228.

33. Lawson, James G. *Deeper Experiences of Famous Christians* (New Kensington, PA: Whitaker House, 1998), 228.

34. Booth, William. Founder of the Salvation Army (Who Cares) Online Source http//:hellwrecker.com/who_cares.htm.

RESOURCES

Ravenhill, Leonard. "George Whitefield: Portrait of a Revival Preacher." *DaySpring: Bethany House Publishers.* 24 Oct. 2003. http://www.ravenhill.org/whitefield.htm.

Unknown. "George Whitefield, 1714-1770, English Evangelist." *Believers Web* CCN 13 March 2003. 24 Oct 2003. http://www.believersweb.org/view.cfm?ID94.

Unknown. "George Whitefield 1774-1770" *The Anglican Library.* 3 Dec. 2003. http://www.anglicanlibrary.org/whitefield.

Smithers, David. "Evan Roberts: Prayer Makes History" *The Watchword: A Revival Resource Center,* Copyright 2003. 24 Oct 2003. http://www.watchword.org/smithers/ww25.html.

Smithers, David. "Charles G. Finney: Prayer Makes History" *The Watchword: A Revival Resource Center.* Copyright 2003. 24 Oct. 2003. http://www.watchword.org/smithers /ww33a.html.

Unknown. "Evan Roberts 1878-1950." 24 Oct 2003. http://www.cantonbaptist.org/halloffame/roberts.html

Finney, Charles G., "The Autobiography of Charles G. Finney-Beginning of My Work." *Biographies-Christians Unite.* 14 Nov. 2003. http://bible.christiansunite.com/charles_finney/finney03.shtml.

Orentas, Dr. Rimas J. "George Whitefield: Lightning rod of the Great Awakening." *Shippensburg UBF. A Symposium on Spiritual Leaders.* 3 Dec. 2003. http://dylee.keel.econ.shi.edu/UBF/leaders/whitfild.htm.

Smithers, David. "John Wesley: Prayer Makes History." *The Watchword: A Revival Resource Center.* Copyright 2003. 24 Oct. 2003. http://www.watchword.org/smithers/ww31a.html.

Whitefield, George. "Sermon 38: The Indwelling of the Spirit, The Common Privilege of All Believers." *Pioneer Net 3.* Dec. 2003. http://www.pioneernet/rbrannan/whitefield/sermons /WITF_038.HTM.

Wesley, John. "Sermon 104 On Attending the Church Service on the Holy Spirit." 24 Oct 2003. http://www.raptureme.com/resource/wesley/serm_104.html.

Unknown. "Martin Luther Brief Biography-Lutherstadt, Wittenberg." 14 Nov. 2003. http://www.wittenbirg.de/e/seiten/personen/luther.html.

CONTACT INFORMATION

TOMMIE ZITO MINISTRIES
P.O. Box 226377
Miami, Florida 33122

Web: www.tommiezito.com

E-mail: info@tommiezito.com

 is a training ground for the radical of heart who have an unceasing desire to see the nation of America shaken one person at a time. It is for those who have come to the realization that their lives can impact a lost world for Christ.

 desires to raise up an army of revolutionaries who are unashamed of the Gospel and passionate for the God they serve. It will be an army of men and women prepared to share the message of Jesus Christ at all costs.

 is for a people so inundated with the message of God's Word that they will stop at nothing short of sharing that same Gospel message to lives waiting to receive a touch from Heaven.

 students will be trained how to infiltrate every aspect of the culture to pierce the darkness with the Light of the world.

Miami Beach will be dispersed with hundreds of individuals delivering the message of love and forgiveness for the lost. The sphere of influence for  students will be unheard of. With this training one will be equipped to carry this revolution throughout the entire nation.

If you are interested in receiving information about , contact us at:

P.O. Box 226377 • Miami, FL 33122

Prepare to live the extraordinary life God calls you to!

Additional copies of this book and other
book titles from DESTINY IMAGE are
available at your local bookstore.

For a bookstore near you, call 1-800-722-6774

Send a request for a catalog to:

Destiny Image® Publishers, Inc.
P.O. Box 310
Shippensburg, PA 17257-0310

"Speaking to the Purposes of God for This
Generation and for the Generations to Come"

For a complete list of our titles,
visit us at www.destinyimage.com